COLOSSAL COLLECTION

Sight Words

D1090263

Newmark Learning
145 Huguenot Street • New Rochelle, NY • 10801

ISBN 978-1-4788-6126-3

For ordering information, call Toll-Free 1-877-279-8388 or visit our website at www.newmarklearning.com.

Table of Contents

Activity Pages

Sight Words 61–80

Sight Words 81–90

Introduction

Colossal Collection: Sight Words includes hundreds of fun, meaningful activities to help children develop and strengthen their recognition of the top 90 high-frequency words from the Dolch Basic Sight Word Vocabulary List. Each page targets a specific sight word and includes activities such as:

- tracing and writing the word
- recognizing the word in isolation
- completing the word spelling
- reading the word in context
- writing the word in context
- unscrambling letters to spell the word

The activity pages can be used with the whole class, small groups, student partners, and individuals. You might use them as part of your lessons on sight words, or have children complete the pages in a learning center, as individual seatwork, or for take-home practice to reinforce what they have learned in class.

Meeting the Standards

The activities in this book also support children in meeting the following Common Core State Standards for Reading Foundational Skills:

- **Print Concepts:** Demonstrate understanding of the organization and basic features of print.
- **Phonological Awareness:** Demonstrate understanding of spoken words, syllables, and sounds.
- **Phonics and Word Recognition:** Read common high-frequency words by sight.
- **Fluency:** Read with sufficient accuracy and fluency to support comprehension.

(For more information, visit www.corestandards.org.)

Using the Activities

The activities in this resource give children lots of opportunities to recognize, read, and write the first 90 words of the Dolch Basic Sight Word Vocabulary List. Each word is featured on two pages with picture clues that provide context to help children read and understand the sentences on the pages.

To use, make a copy of the page(s) for the sight word you want to teach. If you plan to use the activity in a learning center, put the pages in a manila folder and place in the center. The only materials children need to complete the pages are pencils and crayons (or colored pencils). The examples at right represent the different kinds of activities found in the book.

Tips for Using the Activities

- Demonstrate how to complete each kind of activity before having children do it independently.

- Introduce the target word, giving children a warm-up lesson, if needed, to prepare them for doing the activity.

- Monitor children as they complete the activities, offering guidance and correction where needed.

- Distribute copies of pages 7 and 8 to give children additional practice in writing uppercase and lowercase letters.

- Provide additional help to English-language learners. If needed, work individually with these children.

- Use the answer key on pages 189–208 to check children's pages. (Note that each picture that should be colored is shaded with a gray box.)

Activity Page Examples

page 9

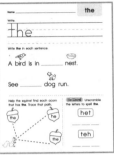
page 10

page 11

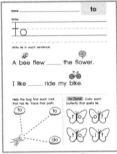
page 12

page 17

page 18

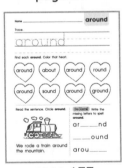
page 177

page 178

Uppercase Letter Formation Practice

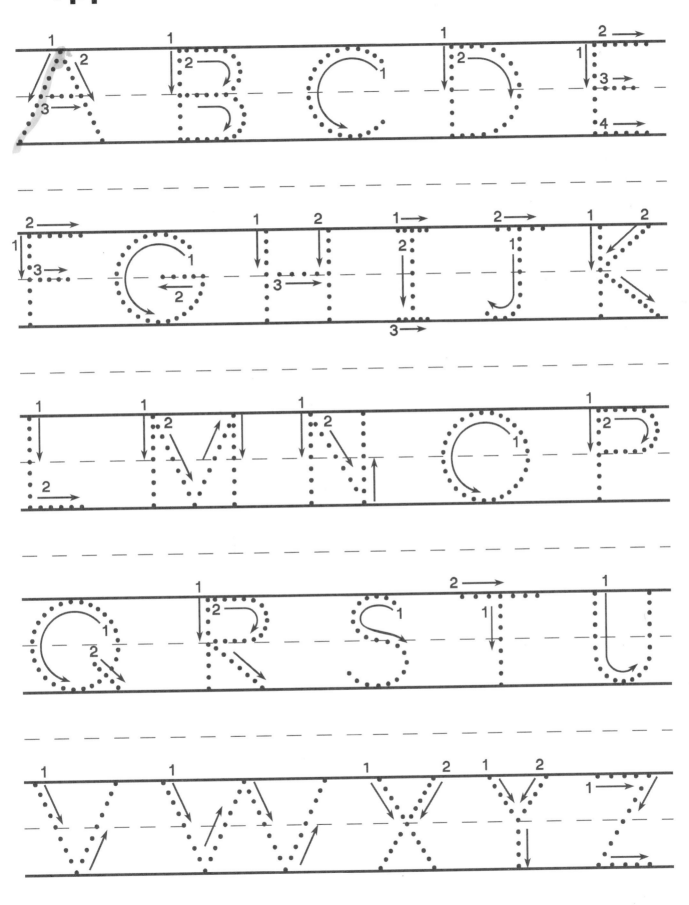

Lowercase Letter Formation Practice

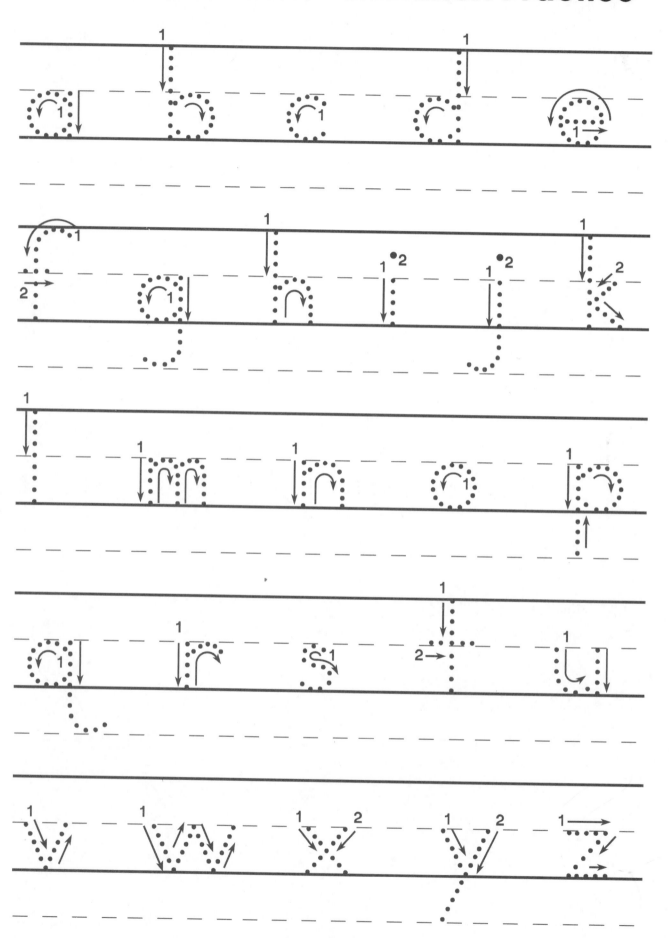

Colossal Collection: Sight Words © Newmark Learning, LLC

Name _____

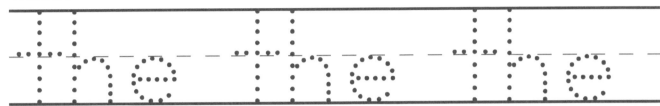
the

Trace.

Find each **the**. Color that apple.

the   the   she   to

with   her   then   the

Read the sentence. Circle **the**.

Some toys are in the box.

Do More! Write the missing letters to spell **the**.

th e

_the

t_e

Colossal Collection: Sight Words © Newmark Learning, LLC   **9**

Name _____

Write.

The

Write **the** in each sentence.

A bird is in _____ nest.

See _____ dog run.

Help the squirrel find each acorn
that has **the**. Trace that path.

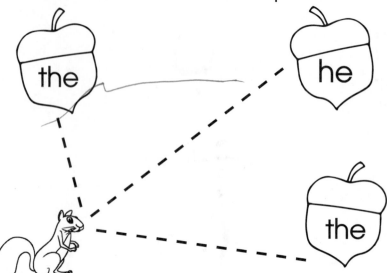

Do More! Unscramble
the letters to spell **the**.

het

_____

teh

_____

Name _____

Trace.

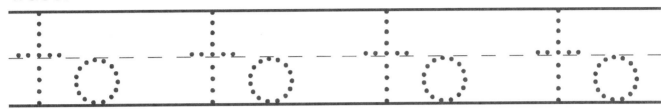

Find each **to**. Color that can.

| of | to | on | to |

| the | at | to | to |

Read the sentence. Circle **to**.

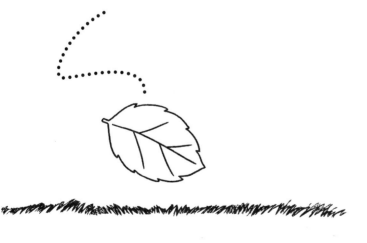

A leaf fell to the ground.

 Do More! Write the missing letters to spell **to**.

t ___   ___ o

___ o   t ___

t ___   ___ o

Name _____

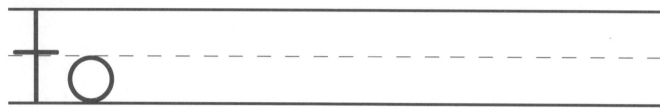

to

Write.

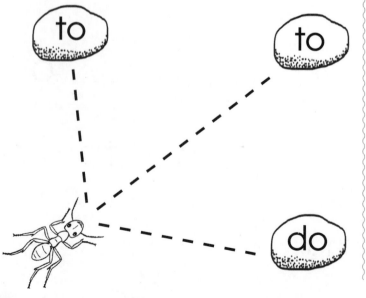

Write **to** in each sentence.

 A bee flew _____ the flower.

I like _____ ride my bike.

Help the bug find each rock that has **to**. Trace that path.

to   to

do

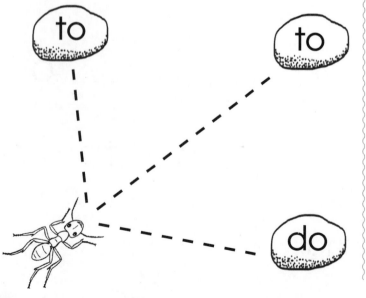

Do More! Color each butterfly that spells **to**.

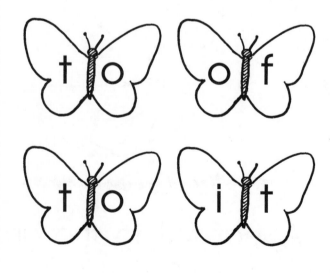

Name _____

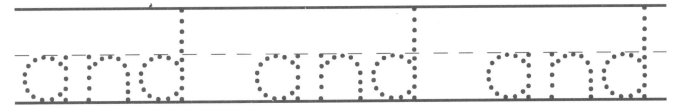

and

Trace.

a n d   a n d   a n d

Find each **and**. Color that cloud.

at

and

ask

and

all

and

and

and

Read the sentence. Circle **and**.

The cat and dog
are friends.

Do More! Write the
missing letters to spell **and**.

___nd

an___

a___d

Name _____

Write.

Write **and** in each sentence.

I like apples _____ bananas.

We have a car _____ a van.

Color each balloon that has **and**. Trace that string.

am   and   and

Do More! Unscramble the letters to spell **and**.

nda

_____

dan

Name _____

he

Trace.

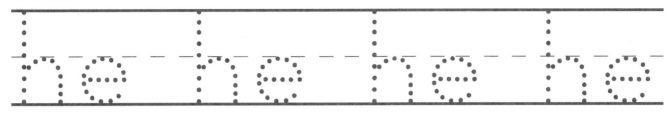

Find each **he**. Color that boot.

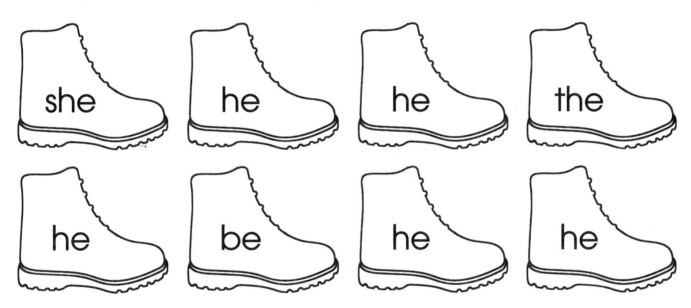

she   he   he   the

he   be   he   he

Read the sentence. Circle **he**.

What did he give
the dog?

Do More! Write the
missing letters to spell **he**.

____e   ____e

h____   ____e

h____   h____

Write.

he

Write he in each sentence.

Did _____ jump into the pool?

I want the same book _____ has.

Help the bird find each tree that has **he**. Trace that path.

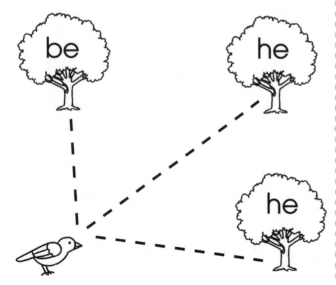

Do More! Color each pair of socks that spells **he**.

Name _____

Trace.

Find each **a**. Color that peach.

Read the sentence. Circle **a**.

I have a new hat!

Do More! Write **a** on each line. Read the phrase.

___ car

___ bus

___ plane

Name _____

Write.

Write **a** in each sentence.

That is _____ funny clown!

I see _____ tall giraffe.

Help the bear find each jar that has **a**. Trace that path.

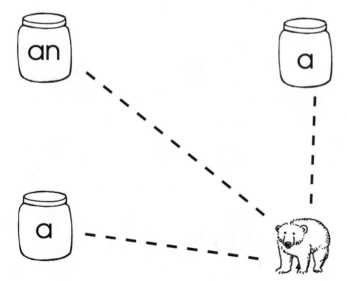

Do More! Circle each **a** in the puzzle.

e a c o n
a b q h e
d o i f a
u p a g o
r a n i s

Name _____

Trace.

_ _

Find each **I**. Color that vase.

Read the sentence. Circle **I**.

I like to pick flowers.

Do More! Write **I** on each line. Read the sentence.

____ eat.

____ drink.

____ play.

Name _____

Write.

Write **I** in each sentence.

_____ want ice cream.

Look! _____ got a gift today!

Help the kid find each jar that has **I**. Trace that path.

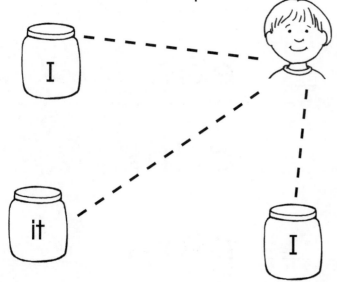

Do More! Circle each **I** in the puzzle.

s	o	t	I	l
I	d	f	b	e
h	j	I	a	t
a	s	o	n	I
r	r	I	k	o	y

Name _____

Trace.

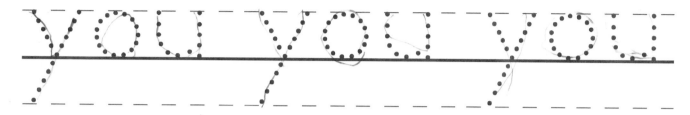

Find each **you**. Color that piggy bank.

us   yes   you   you

you   how   up   you

Read the sentence. Circle **you**.

Do you like to swing?

Do More! Write the missing letters to spell **you**.

___ o u

y ___ u

___ o ___

Name _____

Write.

you

Write **you** in each sentence.

I saw _____ at the store.

Here is a coat for _____.

Help each duck that has **you** get to the pond. Trace that path.

Do More! Unscramble the letters to spell **you**.

oyu

_ _ _

uoy

_ _ _

Name _____

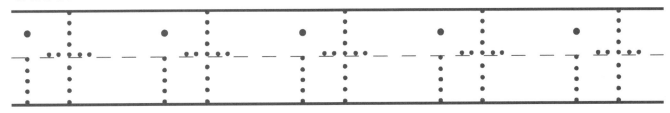

it

Trace.

Find each **it**. Color that cap.

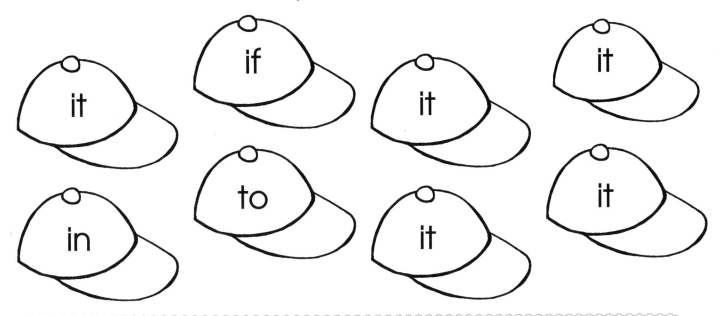

Read the sentence. Circle **it**.

Look at it snow!

Do More! Write the missing letters to spell **it**.

___t   i___

i___   ___t

i___   ___t

Name _____

 it

Write.

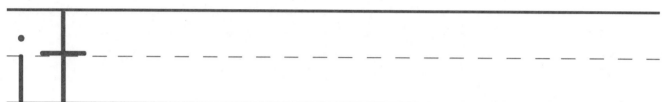

Write **it** in each sentence.

What time is _____?

Pick an apple and eat _____.

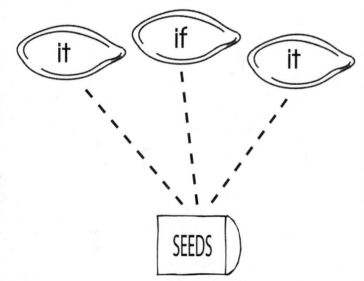

Put each seed that has **it** in the packet. Trace that path.

it

if

it

SEEDS

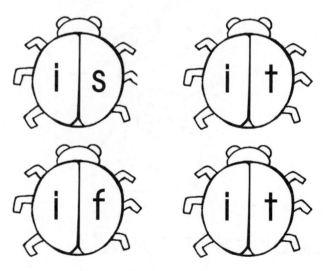

Do More! Color each ladybug that spells **it**.

i s

i t

i f

i t

Name _____

Trace.

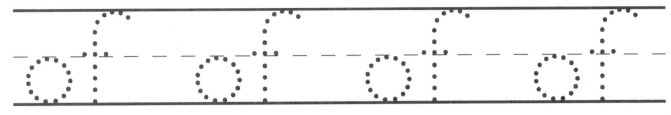

Find each **of**. Color that sock.

of   on   to   of

of   it   of   of

Read the sentence. Circle **of**.

The girl has a lot
of books.

Do More! Write the
missing letters to spell **of**.

___ f   ___ f

o ___   o ___

o ___   ___ f

Name _____

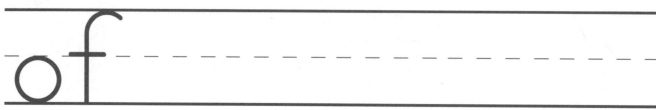

of

Write.

of — — — — — — — — — — — —

— — — — — — — — — — — —

Write **of** in each sentence.

We made a pot _____ soup.

I made a house _____ blocks.

Help each butterfly that has **of** get to the flower. Trace that path.

Do More! Color each pair of pears that spells **of**.

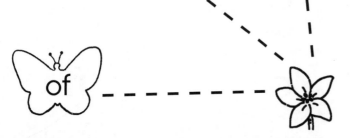

Trace.

Find each **in**. Color that flower.

Read the sentence. Circle **in**.

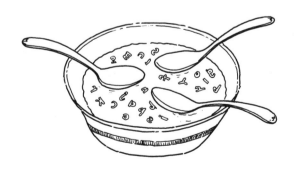

Three spoons are in
my bowl.

Do More! Write the
missing letters to spell **in**.

___n   i___

i___   ___n

i___   ___n

Name _____

Write.

in
- - - - - - - - - - - - - - - - - - - -

Write **in** in each sentence.

A mouse is _____ the house.

I put the ball _____ a basket.

Help each chick that has **in** get to the nest. Trace that path.

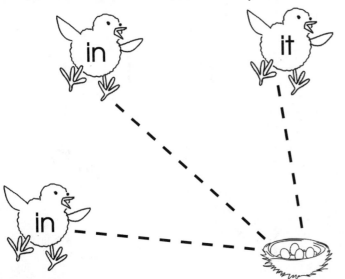

Do More! Color each pair of glasses that spells **in**.

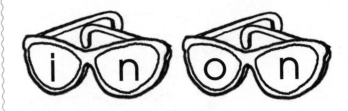

Name _____

Trace.

Find each **was**. Color that clam.

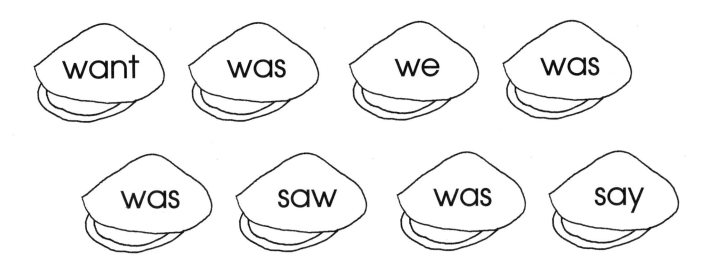

want	was	we	was
was	saw	was	say

Read the sentence. Circle **was**.

The baby was crawling
away fast.

Do More! Write the
missing letters to spell **was**.

w ___ s

___ a s

w a ___

Name _____

was

Write.

_____

 was _____

Write **was** in each sentence.

A girl _____ on the slide.

The plane _____ in the clouds.

Help the frog find each lily pad that has **was**. Trace that path.

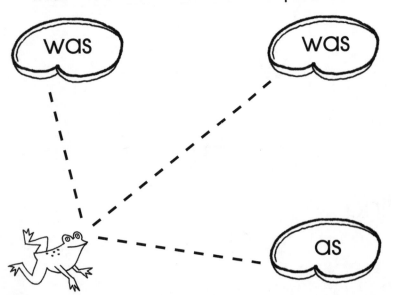

was   was

as

Do More! Unscramble the letters to spell **was**.

saw

___ ___ ___

wsa

Name _____

said

Trace.

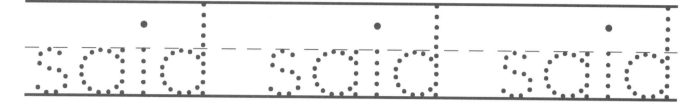

Find each **said**. Color that snail.

Read the sentence. Circle **said**.

Our teacher said we could play games.

Do More! Write the missing letters to spell **said**.

s a ___ d

s ___ ___ d

___ ___ i ___

Name _____

Write.

said

Write **said** in each sentence.

Dad _____ I can fly my kite.

The kids _____ they want cookies.

Help each whale that has **said** get to the water. Trace that path.

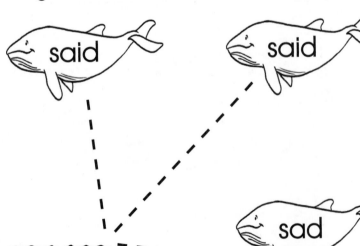

Do More! Unscramble the letters to spell **said**.

sdia

__ __ __ __

aisd

__ __ __ __

Name _____

Trace.

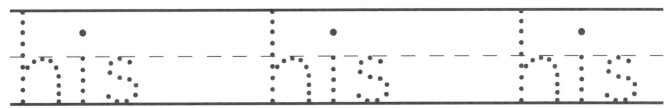

Find each **his**. Color that log.

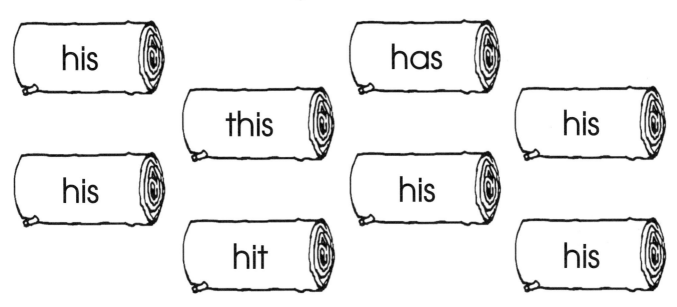

his

this

his

hit

has

his

his

his

Read the sentence. Circle **his**.

The man took a nap
on his couch.

Do More! Write the
missing letters to spell **his**.

h ___ s

___ i s

h _____

Write.

Write **his** in each sentence.

He gave _____ dog a bone.

The prince put on _____ crown.

Help the monkey find each leaf that has **his**. Trace that path.

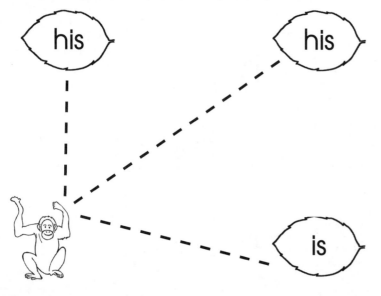

Do More! Unscramble the letters to spell **his**.

hsi

_ _ _

sih

_ _ _

Name _____

Trace.

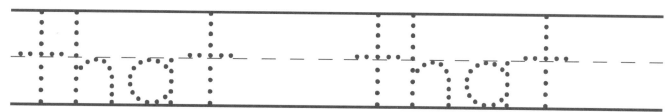

Find each **that**. Color that boat.

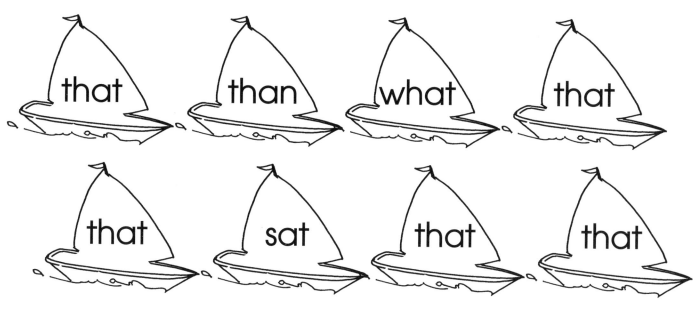

that   than   what   that

that   sat   that   that

Read the sentence. Circle **that**.

Why is that girl yelling?

Do More! Write the missing letters to spell **that**.

t ___ ___ t

___ h a ___

t ___ a ___

Name _____

Write.

t h a t

Write **that** in each sentence.

Can I have _____ pie?

I rode _____ fast train!

Help the horse find each apple that has **that**. Trace that path.

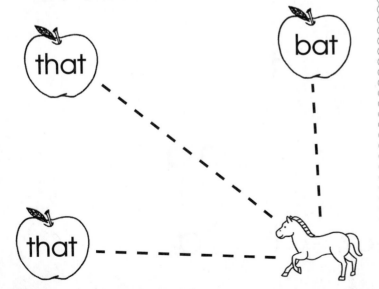

Do More! Unscramble the letters to spell **that**.

htat

_____

atth

_____

Name _____

Trace.

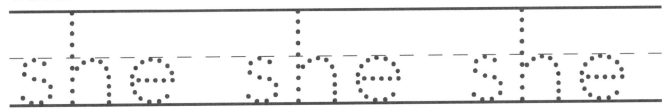

Find each **she**. Color that hen.

Read the sentence. Circle **she**.

I like the shirt she
has on.

Do More! Write the
missing letters to spell **she**.

sh___

s___e

___he

Name _____

Write.

she

Write **she** in each sentence.

Liz said _____ has a pretty hat.

Where did _____ put her purse?

Help the mouse find each peach that has **she**. Trace that path.

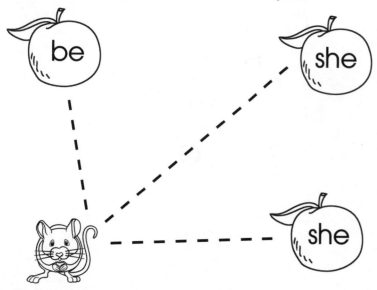

Do More! Unscramble the letters to spell **she**.

seh

_____

ehs

_____

Name _____

Trace.

for for for for

Find each **for**. Color that owl.

for   for   of   or

for   to   four   for

Read the sentence. Circle **for**.

I have a gift for you.

Do More! Write the missing letters to spell **for**.

f___r

___or

fo___

Name _____

for

Write.

for

Write **for** in each sentence.

I got this quilt _____ my bed.

Hold these books _____ me.

Help the bee find each flower that has **for**. Trace that path.

Do More! Unscramble the letters to spell **for**.

rfo

_ _ _

orf

_ _ _

Name _____

on

Trace.

Find each **on**. Color that pan.

one   on   on   won

on   an   on   off

Read the sentence. Circle **on**.

The cat is on the box.

Do More! Write the missing letters to spell **on**.

___n   o___

o___   ___n

___n   o___

Name _____

Write.

on

Write **on** in each sentence.

The bag is _____ the chair.

I put flowers _____ the table.

Help the fox find each box that has **on**. Trace that path.

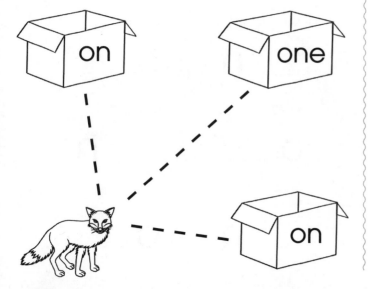

Do More! Color each foot that spells **on**.

Name _____

they

Trace.

Find each **they**. Color that bus.

they   they   they   the

they   them   then   they

Read the sentence. Circle **they**.

Did they get into
our food?

Do More! Write the missing letters to spell **they**.

th_____

t___e___

_____ey

Name _____

Write.

Write **they** in each sentence.

We hope _____ like cake.

Gus said _____ had ice cream.

Help the sheep find each bale of hay that has **they**. Trace that path.

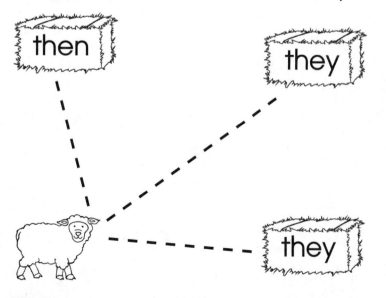

Do More! Unscramble the letters to spell **they**.

| yhet |

_____ _____ _____ _____

| teyh |

_____ _____ _____ _____

Name _____

but

Trace.

Find each **but**. Color that yo-yo.

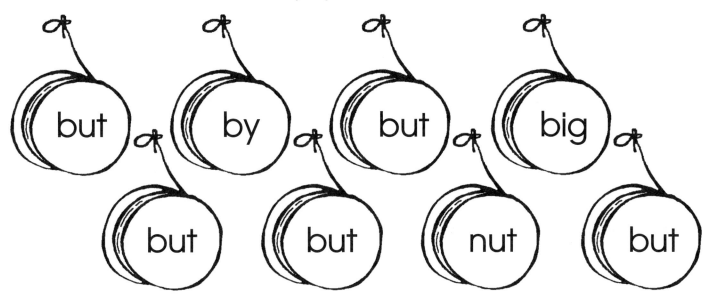

but   by   but   big

but   but   nut   but

Read the sentence. Circle **but**.

I have one cookie,
but I will share.

Do More! Write the
missing letters to spell **but**.

___ut

b___t

bu___

Name _____

Write.

but

Write **but** in each sentence.

We have milk _____ no cookies.

I saw a fish _____ not a shark.

Help the man find each truck that has **but**. Trace that path.

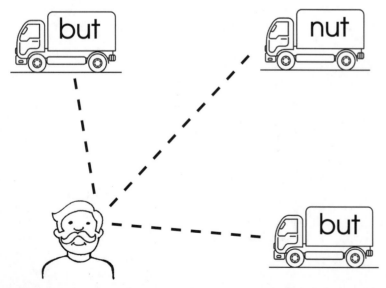

Do More! Unscramble the letters to spell **but**.

tub

_____

btu

_____

Name _____

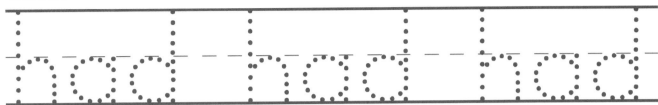

Trace.

ħɑd ħɑd ħɑd

Find each **had**. Color that star.

has had and had

had had bad dad

Read the sentence. Circle **had**.

We had a good time at the zoo.

Do More! Write the missing letters to spell **had**.

h___d

___ad

ha___

Name _____

Write.

had

Write **had** in each sentence.

I _____ lunch at school.

The dog _____ a big bone.

Help the rabbit find each stump that has **had**. Trace that path.

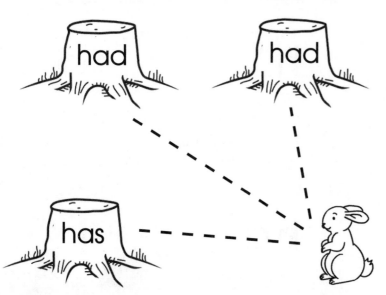

Do More! Unscramble the letters to spell **had**.

dah

_____ _____ _____

hda

_____ _____ _____

Name _____

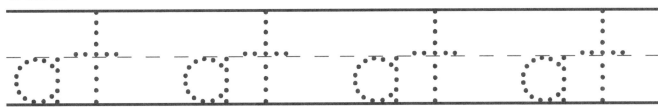
at

Trace.

at at at at

Find each **at**. Color that jar.

all   at   at   an

ate   add   at   at

Read the sentence. Circle **at**.

Jim likes to paint
at his easel.

Do More! Write the
missing letters to spell **at**.

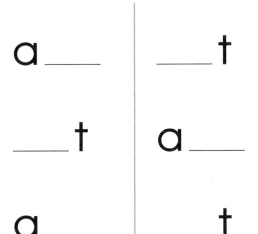

a___   ___t

___t   a___

a___   ___t

Name _____

at

Write.

a t

Write **at** in each sentence.

I got a book _____ the library.

We played ball _____ the park.

Help each fish that has **at** get to the fishbowl. Trace that path.

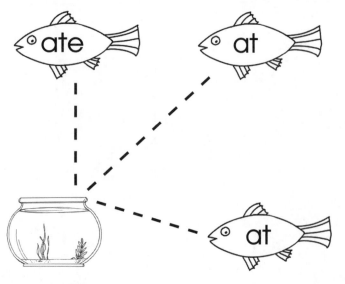

Do More! Color each bird that spells **at**.

Name _____

Trace.

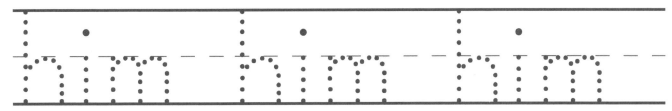

Find each **him**. Color that cup.

his   him   he   him

him   hit   him   hid

Read the sentence. Circle **him**.

We saw him playing
with a yo-yo.

Do More! Write the
missing letters to spell **him**.

hi___

___im

h___m

Name _____

Write.

Write **him** in each sentence.

Please give _____ some juice.

This wagon is for _____ .

Help the deer find each tree that has **him**. Trace that path.

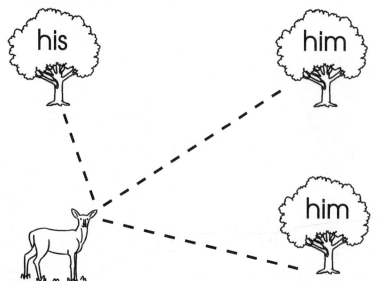

Do More! Unscramble the letters to spell **him**.

| hmi |

_ _ _

| mhi |

_ _ _

Name _____

with

Trace.

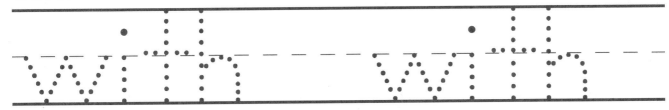

Find each **with**. Color that peach.

Read the sentence. Circle **with**.

I took a walk with
my dog.

Do More! Write the
missing letters to spell **with**.

___ith

w___th

wi_____

Name _____

Write.

with

Write **with** in each sentence.

I want milk _____ my cheese.

Come _____ me to the beach.

Help the kid find each sled
that has **with**. Trace that path.

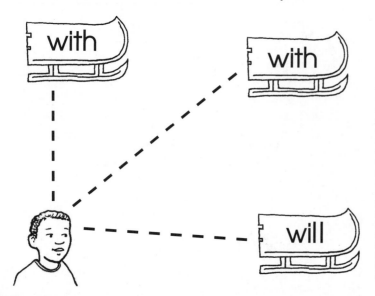
with
with
will

Do More! Unscramble
the letters to spell **with**.

htiw

___ ___ ___ ___

itwh

___ ___ ___ ___

Name _____

Trace.

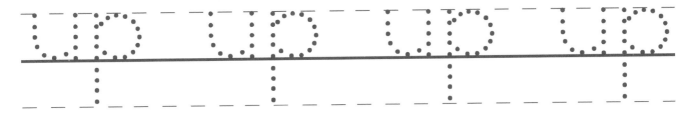

Find each **up**. Color that top.

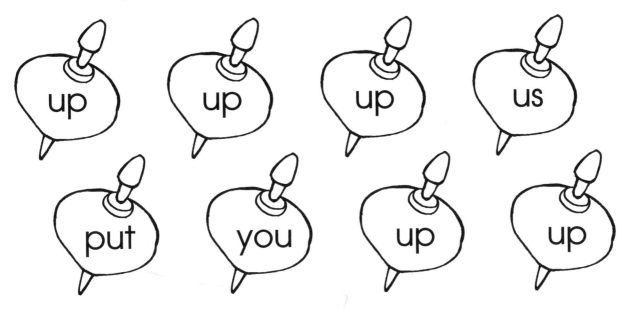

Read the sentence. Circle each **up**.

The kite flew up, up, up!

Do More! Write the missing letters to spell **up**.

u ___   ___ p

___ p   ___ p

u ___   u ___

Name _____

up

Write.

up

Write **up** in each sentence.

Mom ran _____ the stairs.

The bus went _____ the hill.

Help the bug find each rock that has **up**. Trace that path.

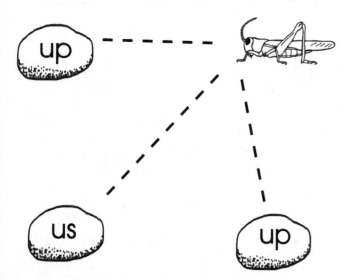

Do More! Color each mitten that spells **up**.

 Colossal Collection: Sight Words © Newmark Learning, LLC

Name _____

Trace.

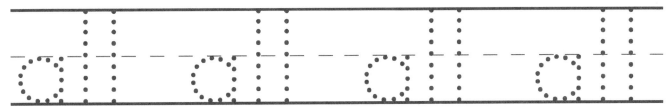

Find each **all**. Color that plate.

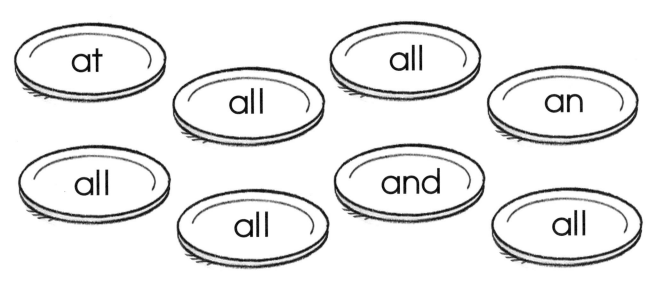

Read the sentence. Circle **all**.

I will eat all of my
ice cream.

Do More! Write the
missing letters to spell **all**.

a ___ l

___ ll

a _____

Name _____

Write.

a l l

Write **all** in each sentence.

Look at _____ of the stars!

We _____ want hot dogs.

Help the baby find each bib that has **all**. Trace that path.

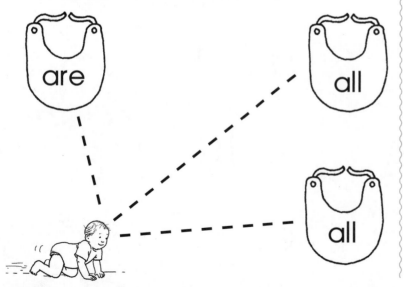

Do More! Unscramble the letters to spell **all**.

lal

_ _ _

lla

_ _ _

Name _____

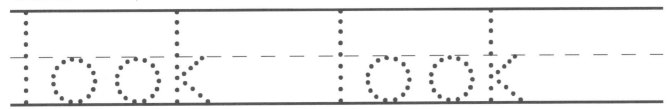

look

Trace.

l o o k   l o o k

Find each **look**. Color that computer.

lock

look

look

like

look

lot

look

too

Read the sentence. Circle **look**.

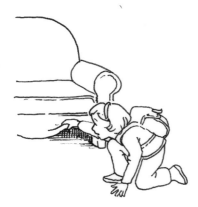

I will look here for
the cat.

Do More! Write the
missing letters to spell **look**.

l __ o k

__ o o __

l ____ k

Name _____

Write.

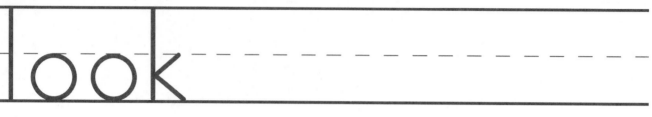

l o o k

Write **look** in each sentence.

I like to _____ at the fish.

Help me _____ for my shoes.

Help the ant find each rock that has **look**. Trace that path.

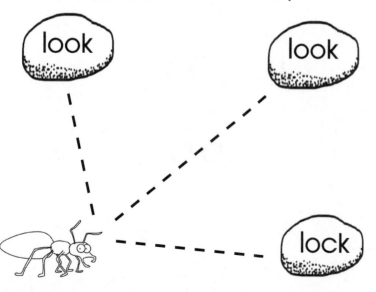

look

look

lock

Do More! Unscramble the letters to spell **look**.

lkoo

_ _ _ _

oklo

_ _ _ _

Name _____

Trace.

Find each **is**. Color that candle.

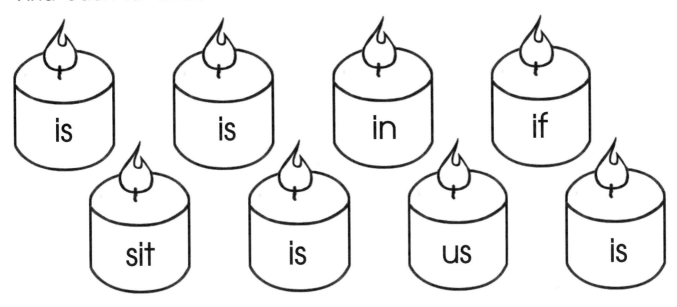

is   is   in   if

sit   is   us   is

Read the sentence. Circle **is**.

A squirrel is in the tree.

Do More! Write the missing letters to spell **is**.

i__   i__

i__   __s

__s   __s

Name _____

Write.

is _____

Write **is** in each sentence.

My cat _____ chasing a mouse.

The cow _____ in the barn.

Help the kid find each bell that has **is**. Trace that path.

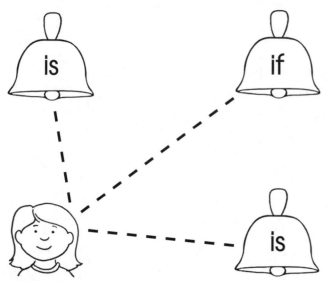

Do More! Color each pair of music notes that spells **is**.

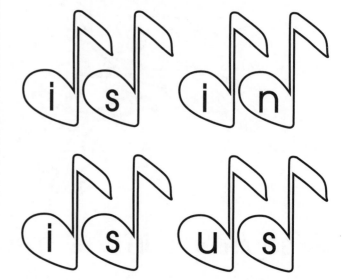

Name _____

Trace.

Find each **her**. Color that ring.

 her    he    her    hen

 her    her    the    here

Read the sentence. Circle **her**.

The girl smiles as she does her yard work.

Do More! Write the missing letters to spell **her**.

___ e r

h ___ r

___ e ___

Name _____

Write.

her

Write **her** in each sentence.

I like to look at _____ picture.

The girl gave me _____ lollipop.

Help the kid find each jar that has **her**. Trace that path.

Do More! Unscramble the letters to spell **her**.

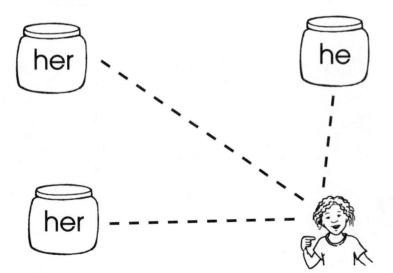

her

he

her

reh

_____ _____ _____

ehr

_____ _____ _____

there

Trace.

there   there

Find each **there**. Color that bed.

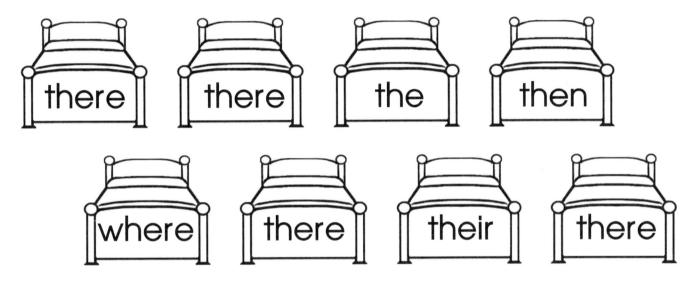

there   there   the   then

where   there   their   there

Read the sentence.
Circle **there**.

The plane is up
there in the sky.

Do More! Write the
missing letters to spell **there**.

the___e

___ ___e___e

th___r___

Name _____

Write.

Write **there** in each sentence.

The pig is _____ in the mud.

Your gift is over _____ .

Help the cow find each bale of hay that has **there**. Trace that path.

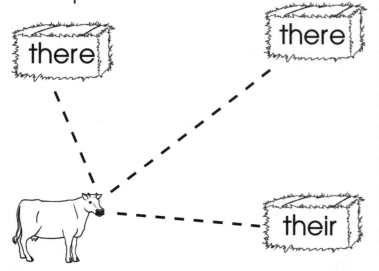

Do More! Unscramble the letters to spell **there**.

hetre

_____

teher

_____

Name _____

some

Trace.

- -

Find each **some**. Color that leaf.

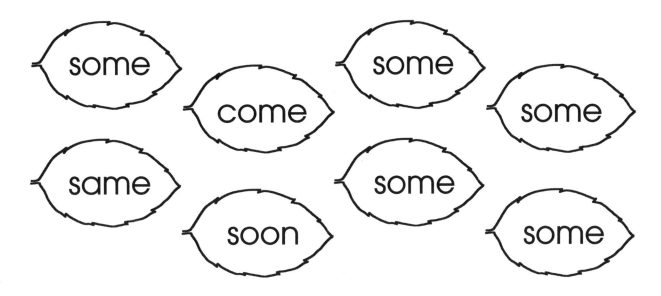

~~~~~~

Read the sentence. Circle **some**.

We made some
posters for our room.

Do More! Write the
missing letters to spell **some**.

s o ___ e

___ o ___ e

s ___ ___ e

Colossal Collection: Sight Words © Newmark Learning, LLC   **67**

Name _____

some

Write.

some

Write **some** in each sentence.

I see _____ eggs in the nest.

Do you want _____ cake?

Help the turtle find each log that has **some**. Trace that path.

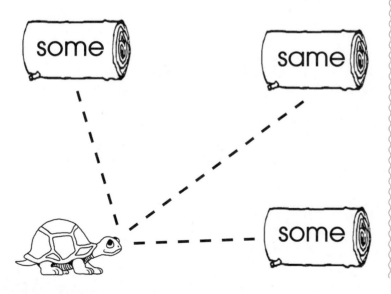

Do More! Unscramble the letters to spell **some**.

meso

_____ _____ _____ _____

oesm

_____ _____ _____ _____

Name _____

out

Trace.

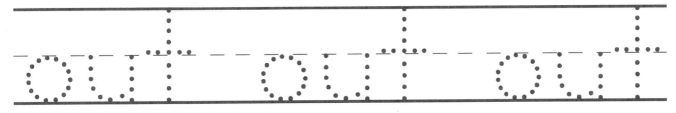

Find each **out**. Color that pie.

out out put our

out but out out

Read the sentence. Circle **out**.

He went out to throw the ball.

Do More! Write the missing letters to spell **out**.

o __ t

ou __

__ ut

Name _____

Write.

out _ _ _ _ _ _ _ _ _ _ _ _ _ _ _ _ _

Write **out** in each sentence.

Dad came _____ of the store.

The bird flew _____ the window.

Help the girl find each bag that has **out**. Trace that path.

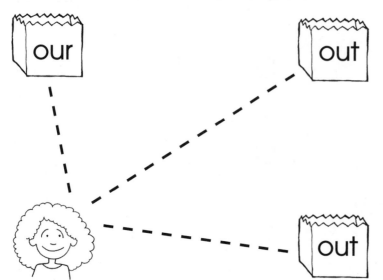

| Do More! | Unscramble the letters to spell **out**.

tou

_ _ _

uto

_ _ _

Name _____

Trace.

Find each **as**. Color that barn.

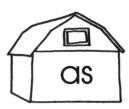 as  ask 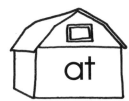 at 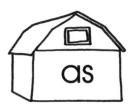 as

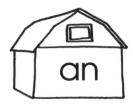 an  as  has 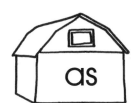 as

Read the sentence. Circle **as**.

We count our steps
as we walk.

Do More! Write the missing letters to spell **as**.

a____   ____s

____s   a____

a____   ____s

Name _____

Write.

as

Write **as** in each sentence.

I jump _____ fast _____ I can!

I sing _____ I sweep the floor.

Help the snowman find each snowflake that has **as**. Trace that path.

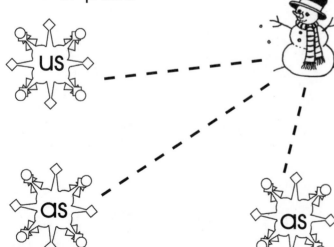

Do More! Color each vest that spells **as**.

Name _____

be

Trace.

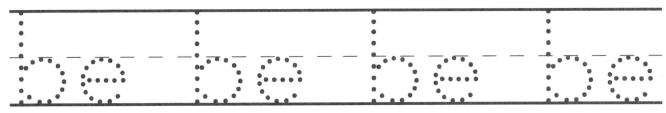

Find each **be**. Color that nest.

 me

 be

 he

 be

 by

 be

 be

 be

Read the sentence. Circle **be**.

He is going to be a good skater.

Do More! Write the missing letters to spell **be**.

__e   __e

b__   b

__e   b

Name _____

Write.

b e

Write **be** in each sentence.

Ducks like to _____ in the water.

I want to _____ a fire fighter.

Help the cow find each barn that has **be**. Trace that path.

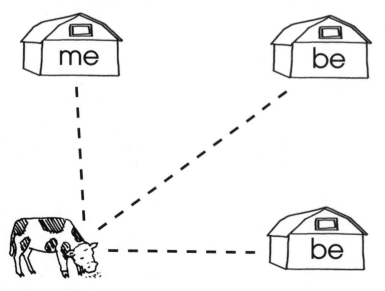

Do More! Color each book that spells **be**.

have

Trace.

have have

Find each **have**. Color that drum.

have   has   have   have

gave   had   have   hat

Read the sentence. Circle **have**.

I have something to tell you.

Do More! Write the missing letters to spell **have**.

ha___ ___

h___ve

___ a ___ e

Name _____

Write.

have

Write **have** in each sentence.

I _____ money for new shoes.

Do you _____ a red crayon?

Help the kid find each bowl that has **have**. Trace that path.

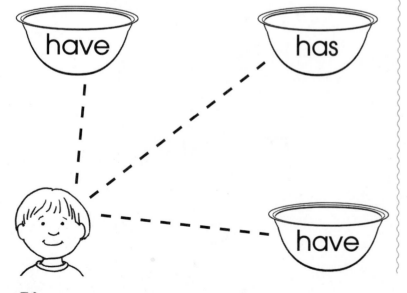

Do More! Unscramble the letters to spell **have**.

ehva

_____

vaeh

_____

Name _____

go

Trace.

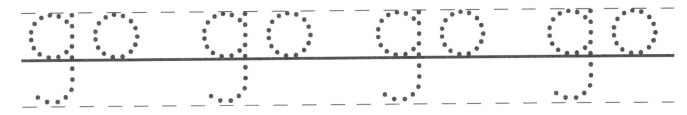

Find each **go**. Color that clam.

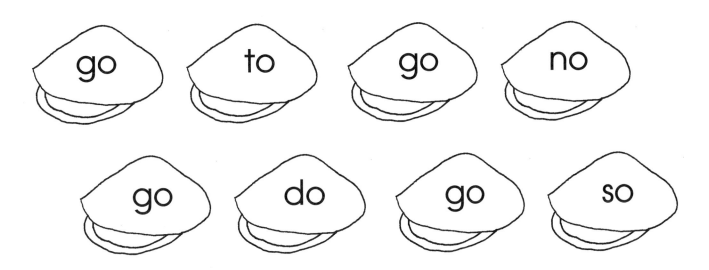

go   to   go   no

go   do   go   so

Read the sentence. Circle **go**.

Where will the aliens go now?

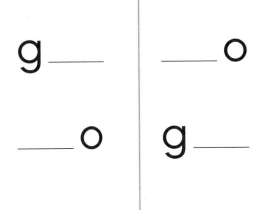
Do More! Write the missing letters to spell **go**.

g___   ___o

___o   g

g___   ___o

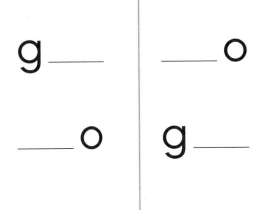

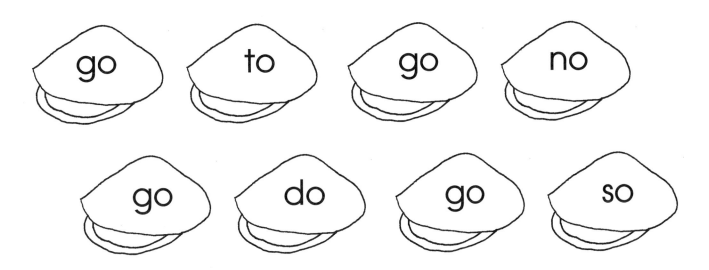

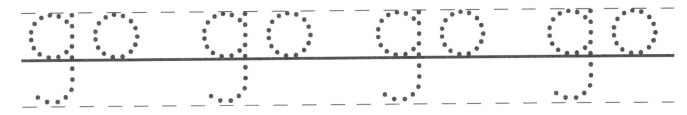

Name _____

Write.

_____

go

Write **go** in each sentence.

We like to _____ to the farm.

I can _____ fast on my bike.

Help the caterpillar find each leaf that has **go**. Trace that path.

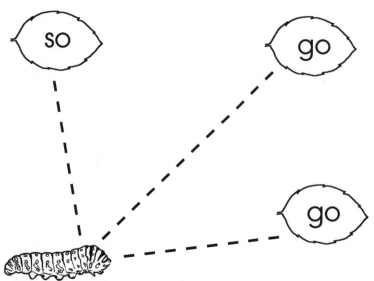

Do More! Color each strawberry that spells **go**.

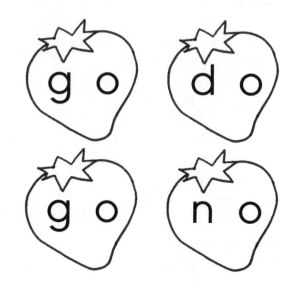

Trace.

Find each **we**. Color that bib.

win

me

we

we

he

we

she

we

Read the sentence. Circle **we**.

Will we see a clown at the circus?

Do More! Write the missing letters to spell **we**.

w ___   ___ e

w ___   ___ e

___ e   w ___

Name _____

Write.

we

Write **we** in each sentence.

Can _____ play this game?

See the beans _____ found!

Help the horse find each apple that has **we**. Trace that path.

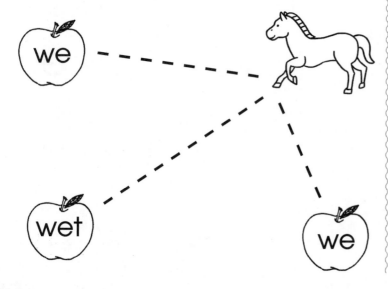

Do More! Color each plate that spells **we**.

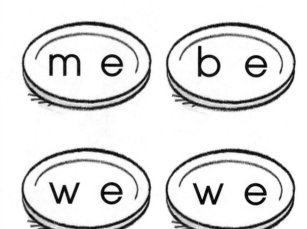

Name _____

Trace.

Find each **am**. Color that sponge.

Read the sentence. Circle **am**.

I am baking a cake.

Do More! Write the missing letters to spell **am**.

a____   ____m

____m   a____

a____   ____m

Name _____

Write.

am

Write **am** in each sentence.

I _____ in my bed now.

I _____ getting my hair cut.

Help the crab find each shell that has **am**. Trace that path.

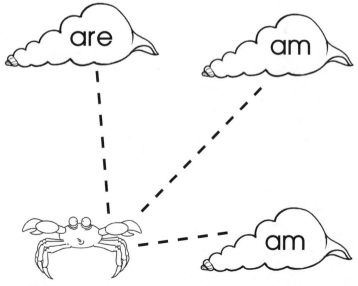

Do More! Color each balloon that spells **am**.

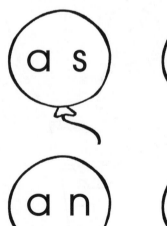
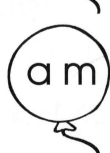

Name _____

Trace.

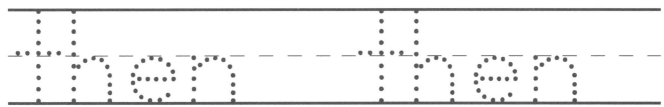

Find each **then**. Color that cake.

Read the sentence. Circle **then**.

Brush, then floss your teeth.

Do More! Write the missing letters to spell **then**.

th___n

_____en

t___e___

Name _____

Write.

Write **then** in each sentence.

Feed the cat, _____ the dog.

Eat lunch, _____ take a cookie.

Help the kid find each book that has **then**. Trace that path.

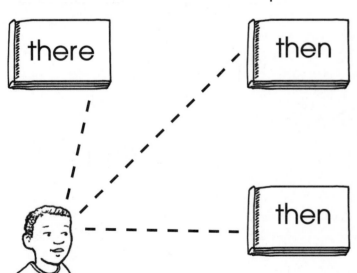

there

then

then

Do More! Unscramble the letters to spell **then**.

nhet

_____

tenh

_____

Name _____

Trace.

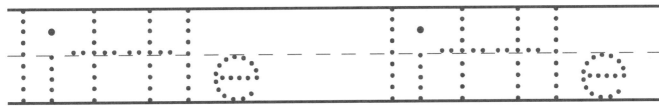

Find each **little**. Color that quail.

live   like   little   little

little   light   little   let

Read the sentence. Circle **little**.

Mary has three little lambs.

Do More! Write the missing letters to spell **little**.

litt_____

_____ttle

li_____le

Name _____

little

Write.

little

Write **little** in each sentence.

A _____ mouse ate the cheese.

A _____ worm was in the plum.

Help the bird find each cloud that has **little**. Trace that path.

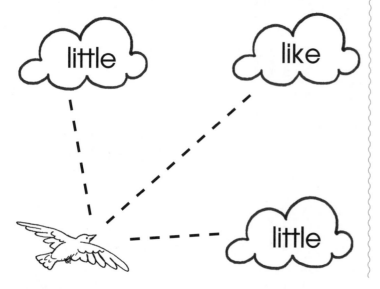

Do More! Unscramble the letters to spell **little**.

tetlil

_ _ _ _ _ _

litelt

_ _ _ _ _ _

86   Colossal Collection: Sight Words © Newmark Learning, LLC

Name _____

Trace.

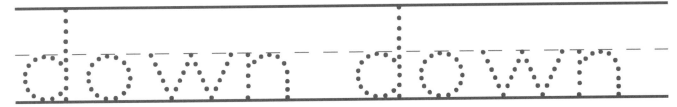

Find each **down**. Color that robot.

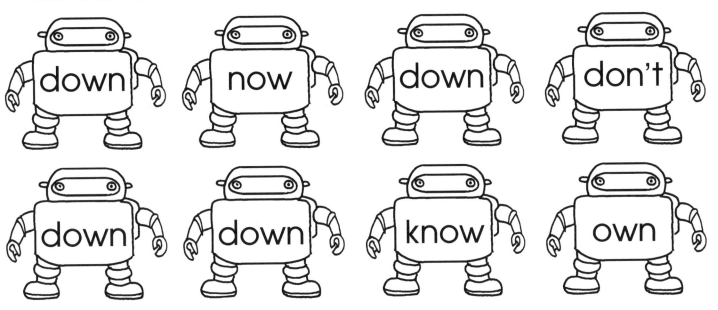

down   now   down   don't

down   down   know   own

Read the sentence. Circle **down**.

The man went down
the hill fast!

Do More! Write the
missing letters to spell
down.

d__wn

__o__n

do____

Name _____

Write.

down

Write **down** in each sentence.

Put the books _____ here.

Let's sit _____ on this bench.

Help the dog find each bone that has **down**. Trace that path.

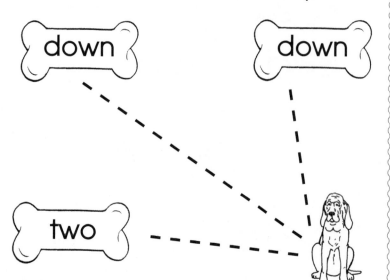

down

down

two

Do More! Unscramble the letters to spell **down**.

nowd

__ __ __ __

donw

__ __ __ __

Name _____

Trace.

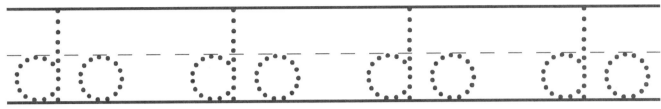

Find each **do**. Color that computer.

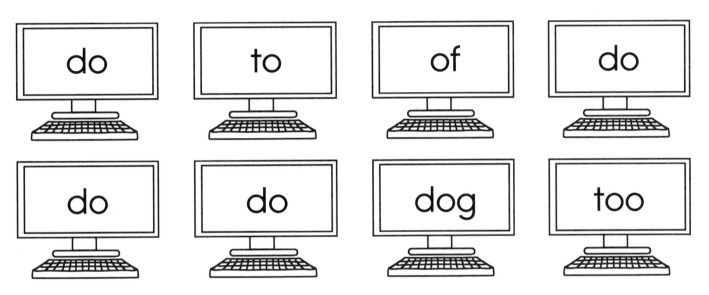

Read the sentence. Circle **do**.

What do you think he is drawing?

 Write the missing letters to spell **do**.

d___   ___o

___o   d___

d___   ___o

Name _____

Write.

Write **do** in each sentence.

What time _____ you go to bed?

Please help me _____ the dishes.

Help the ladybug find each flower that has **do**. Trace that path.

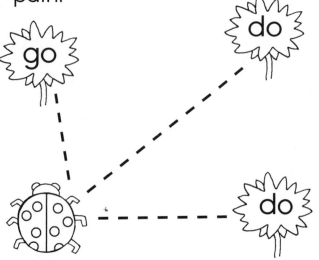

Do More! Color each cube that spells **do**.

Name _____

Trace.

Find each **can**. Color that cow.

and

can

any

can

ran

came

can

can

Read the sentence. Circle **can**.

See how we can pet
the horse.

Do More! Write the
missing letters to spell **can**.

___ a n

c ___ n

___ a ___

Name _____

Write.

can

Write **can** in each sentence.

I _____ button my shirt!

You _____ have this apple.

Help the cook find each can that has **can**. Trace that path.

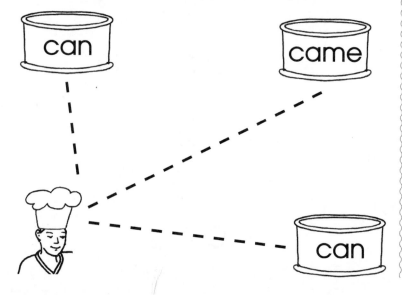

Do More! Unscramble the letters to spell **can**.

cna

_____

acn

_____

Name _____

Trace.

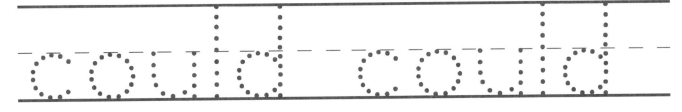

Find each **could**. Color that blimp.

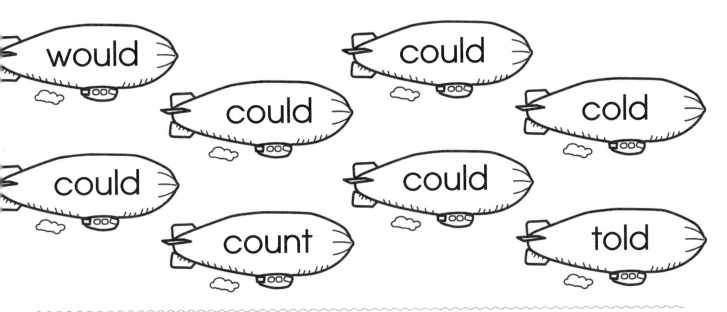

would

could

could

cold

could

could

count

told

Read the sentence. Circle **could**.

Mom said we could
sleep in the tent.

Do More! Write the
missing letters to spell
could.

c ____ ld

cou ___ d

___ oul ___

Name _____

Write.

could

Write **could** in each sentence.

I _____ wear my new hat.

We _____ have soup tonight.

Help the goat find each haystack that has **could**. Trace that path.

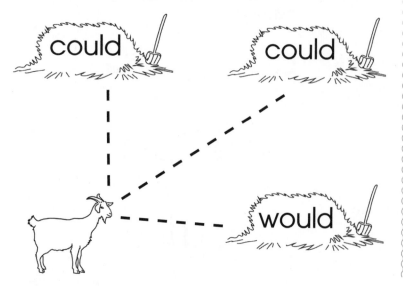

Do More! Unscramble the letters to spell **could**.

dluoc

_____

ocudl

_____

Name _____

Trace.

Find each **when**. Color that cloud.

Read the sentence. Circle **when**.

We will get on the bus when it comes.

Do More! Write the missing letters to spell **when**.

wh___n

_____en

w___e___

Name _____

when

Write.

when

Write **when** in each sentence.

Walk the dog _____ you can.

We play _____ the sun is out.

Help the bug find each rock that has **when**. Trace that path.

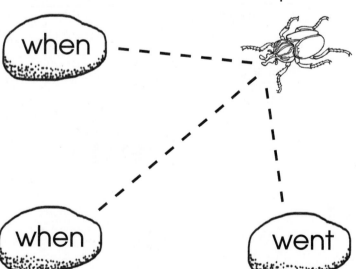

when

when   went

Do More! Unscramble the letters to spell **when**.

henw

__ __ __ __

wehn

__ __ __ __

Name _____

Trace.

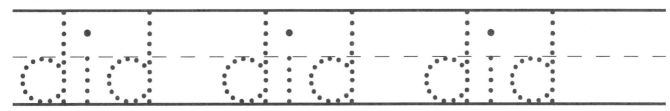

Find each **did**. Color that rock.

did   said   did   dig

did   hid   lid   did

Read the sentence. Circle **did**.

Where did you get your new pants?

Do More! Write the missing letters to spell **did**.

d___d

___id

di___

Name _____

did

Write.

did

Write **did** in each sentence.

How _____ you hurt your knee?

Sam _____ a flip in the pool.

Help the king find each crown that has **did**. Trace that path.

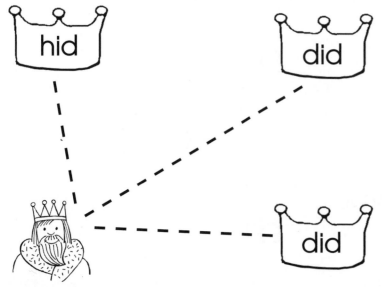

hid

did

did

Do More! Unscramble the letters to spell **did**.

ddi

_ _ _

idd

98   Colossal Collection: Sight Words © Newmark Learning, LLC

Name _____

Trace.

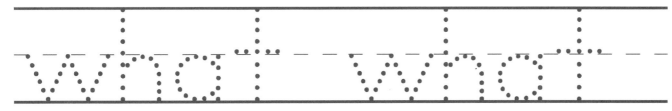

Find each **what**. Color that bale of hay.

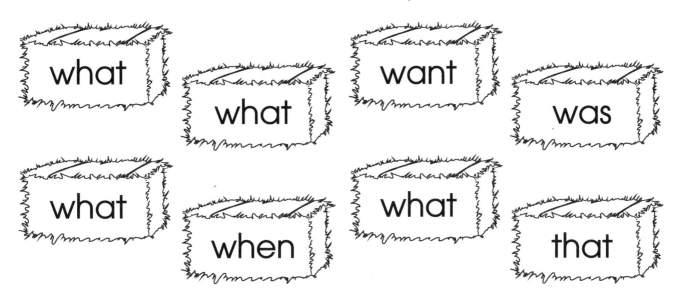

what   what   want   was

what   when   what   that

Read the sentence. Circle **what**.

I know what will come out of the egg.

Do More! Write the missing letters to spell **what**.

w h a ___

___ ___ a t

w h ___ ___ ___

Name _____

Write.

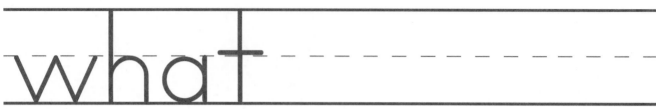

Write **what** in each sentence.

I like _____ she is wearing.

See _____ I have in the box!

Help the clown find each cotton candy that has **what**. Trace that path.

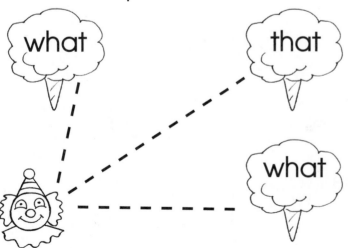

hwta

_____

wath

_____

Name _____

Trace.

Find each **so**. Color that dog house.

Read the sentence. Circle **so**.

The wind is blowing
so hard!

 Write the
missing letters to spell **so**.

S ____	____ O
____ O	S ____
____ O	S ____

Name _____

Write.

SO

Write **so** in each sentence.

A bird flew _____ close to me.

The kids are _____ happy.

Help the rabbit find each
strawberry that has **so**.
Trace that path.

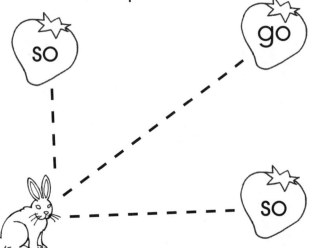

Do More! Color each
bowl that spells **so**.

Name _____

Trace.

Find each **see**. Color that seed.

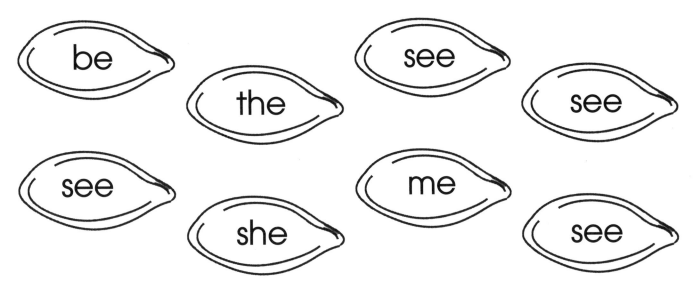

Read the sentence. Circle **see**.

I see the moon in the sky.

Do More! Write the missing letters to spell **see**.

s ___ e

___ e e

s ___ e

Write.

see

Write **see** in each sentence.

Do you _____ the zebra?

I want to _____ all the fish.

Help the elephant find each peanut that has **see**. Trace that path.

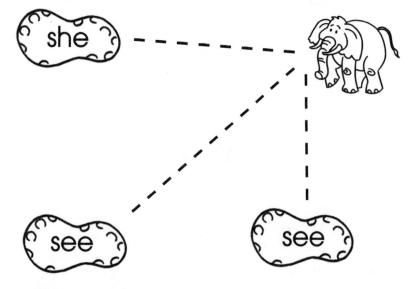

she

see

see

 Unscramble the letters to spell **see**.

ees

___ ___ ___

ese

Name _____

Trace.

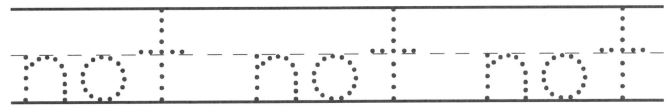

Find each **not**. Color that acorn.

Read the sentence. Circle **not**.

The kitten could not
get out.

Do More! Write the
missing letters to spell **not**.

n___t

___ot

no___

Name _____

Write.

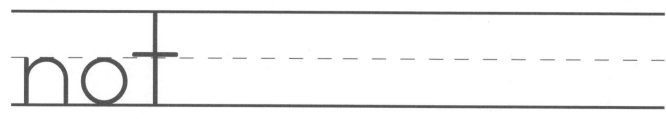

Write **not** in each sentence.

It did _____ rain today.

I did _____ see a whale.

Help the kid find each mitten that has **not**. Trace that path.

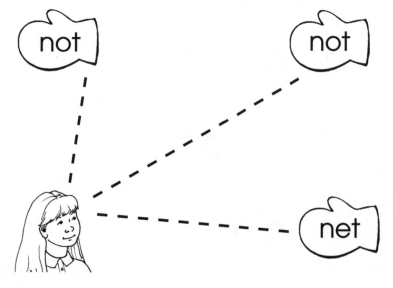

not

not

net

Do More! Unscramble the letters to spell **not**.

ont

_____

ton

_____

Name _____

Trace.

were were

Find each **were**. Color that saw.

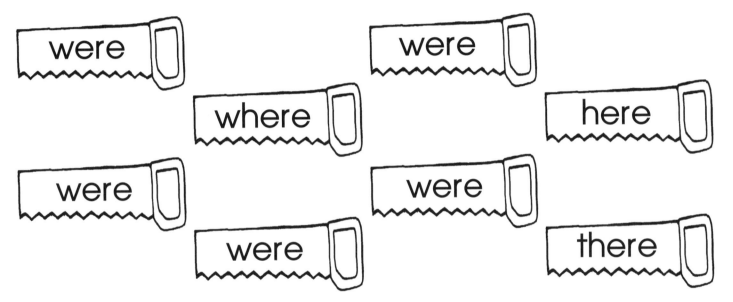

were

where

were

were

were

here

were

there

Read the sentence. Circle **were**.

We were glad our
team won!

Do More! Write the
missing letters to spell **were**.

we___e

___e___e

___er___

Name _____

Write.

were

Write **were** in each sentence.

 Our dogs _____ running fast.

 The pigs _____ in the barn.

Help the frog find each log that has **were**. Trace that path.

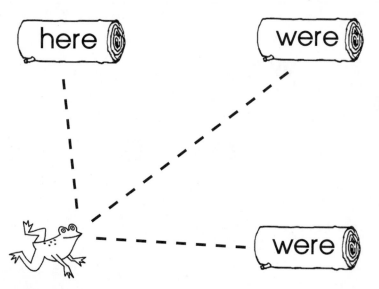

Do More! Unscramble the letters to spell **were**.

weer

_____

rewe

_____

Name _____

Trace.

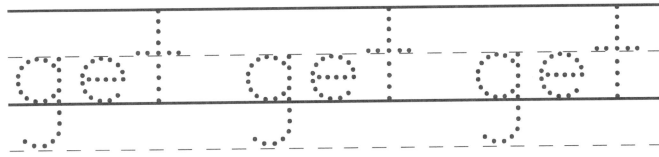

Find each **get**. Color that slice of bread.

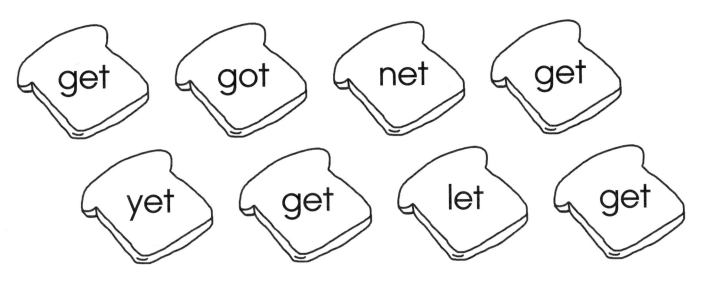

get   got   net   get

yet   get   let   get

Read the sentence. Circle **get**.

Let's get on our bikes and ride.

Do More! Write the missing letters to spell **get**.

___ e t

g ___ t

g e ___

get

Write.

get

Write **get** in each sentence.

I want to _____ some skates.

Did you _____ the letter I sent?

Help the owl find each tree that has **get**. Trace that path.

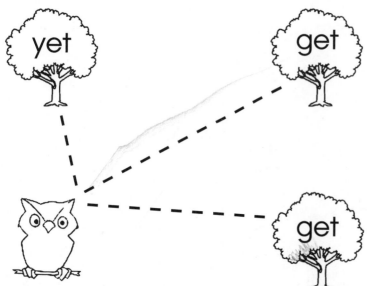

yet   get   get

Do More! Unscramble the letters to spell **get**.

egt

_____

teg

_____

Name _____

Trace.

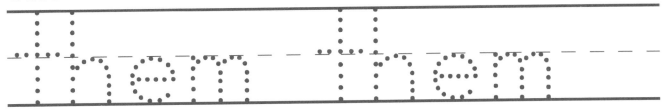

Find each **them**. Color that apple.

them   then   the   them

they   them   there   them

Read the sentence. Circle **them**.

I rode with them to the city.

Do More! Write the missing letters to spell **them**.

th___m

___he___

_____em

Name _____

Write.

Them

Write **them** in each sentence.

I pick berries and eat _____ .

Let's give _____ some grapes.

Help the bug find each rock that has **them**. Trace that path.

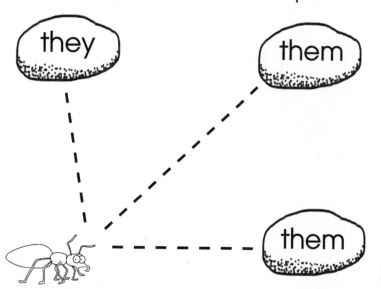

Do More! Unscramble the letters to spell **them**.

mhet

___ ___ ___ ___

temh

___ ___ ___ ___

Name _____

like

Trace.

¦ike ¦ike ¦ike

Find each **like**. Color that sheep.

 like
 like
 lick
 lit

 like
 live
 like
 lid

Read the sentence. Circle **like**.

I like to make things with blocks.

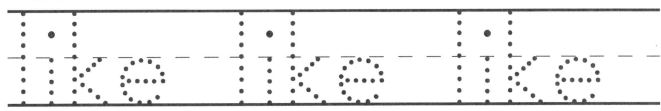
Do More! Write the missing letters to spell **like**.

l__ke

__ik__

l____e

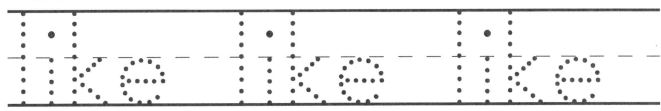

Name _____

like

Write.

like

Write **like** in each sentence.

Do you _____ pizza or hot dogs?

We _____ to jump rope.

Color each balloon that has **like**. Trace that string.

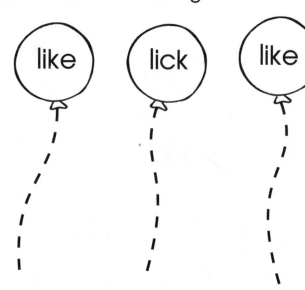

Do More! Unscramble the letters to spell **like**.

| lkie |

_ _ _ _

| ekil |

_ _ _ _

 Colossal Collection: Sight Words © Newmark Learning, LLC

Name _____

Trace.

Find each **one**. Color that whale.

Read the sentence. Circle **one**.

We saw one cloud in the sunny sky.

Do More! Write the missing letters to spell **one**.

on___

___ne

o___e

Name _____

Write.

one

Write **one** in each sentence.

There is _____ ball in the box.

I want _____ cookie.

Help the squirrel find each acorn that has **one**. Trace that path.

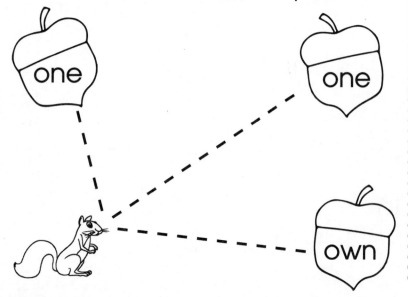

Do More! Unscramble the letters to spell **one**.

| noe |

_____ _____ _____

| eno |

_____ _____ _____

Name _____

Trace.

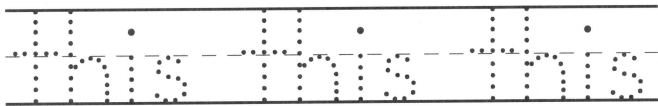

Find each **this**. Color that turtle.

Read the sentence. Circle **this**.

I like this sweater with the dots.

Do More! Write the missing letters to spell **this**.

t_____s

th_____

_____is

Write.

Write **this** in each sentence.

⬭

That egg belongs to _____ hen.

I want _____ puppy for a pet.

Help each duck that has **this** get to the pond. Trace that path.

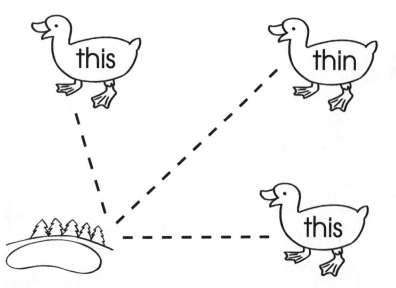

Do More! Unscramble the letters to spell **this**.

hsti

_ _ _ _

ihts

_ _ _ _

Name _____

Trace.

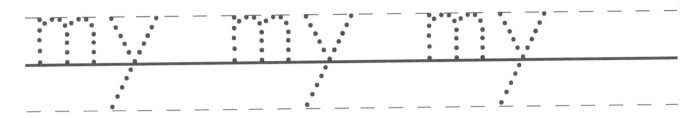

Find each **my**. Color that can.

my	by	me	my

my	may	my	any

Read the sentence. Circle **my**.

You can have some of my pie.

Do More! Write the missing letters to spell **my**.

m___   ___y

___y   m___

___y   m___

Write.

my

Write **my** in each sentence.

You can sit in _____ chair.

Will you help with _____ puzzle?

Help the kid find each bottle that has **my**. Trace that path.

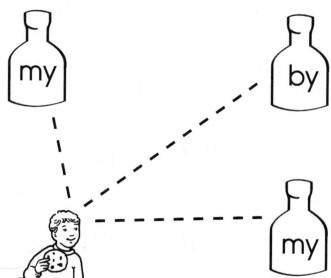

Do More! Color each jar that spells **my**.

Name _____    **would**

Trace.

would would

Find each **would**. Color that sock.

would   would   down   could

world   would   cold   would

Read the sentence. Circle **would**.

What book would you
like to read?

Do More! Write the
missing letters to spell
would.

wo ___ ___ d

___ oul ___

w ___ u ___ d

Name _____

Write.

would

Write **would** in each sentence.

The bear _____ like berries.

I _____ like to be a teacher.

Help the frog find each lily pad that has **would**. Trace that path.

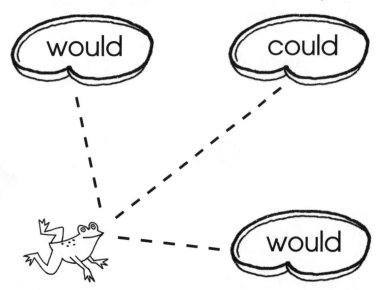

Unscramble the letters to spell **would**.

dluwo

__ __ __ __ __

ulwod

__ __ __ __ __

Name _____

Trace.

Find each **me**. Color that flower.

Read the sentence. Circle **me**.

Please let me play with the ball.

m___ | ___e

___e | m___

m___ | ___e

Name _____

Write.

me

Write **me** in each sentence.

Please pass the crayon to _____.

She gave _____ a toothbrush.

Put each seed that has **me** in the packet. Trace that path.

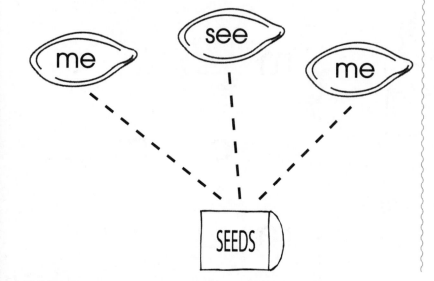

Do More! Color each pear that spells **me**.

Name _____

Trace.

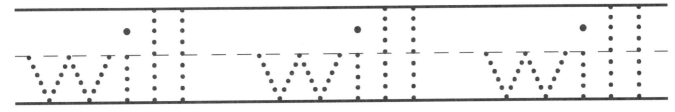

Find each **will**. Color that cap.

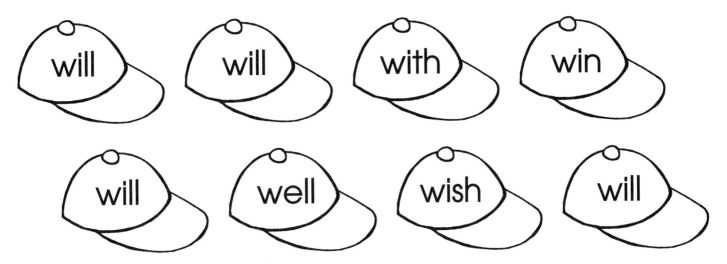

will   will   with   win

will   well   wish   will

~~~~~~

Read the sentence. Circle **will**.

Where will we go on our hike?

Do More! Write the missing letters to spell **will**.

w ____ ll

____ i l ____

____ i ____ l

Name _____

Write.

will

Write **will** in each sentence.

We _____ plant the seeds.

I hope I _____ catch a fish.

Help the bird find each tree that has **will**. Trace that path.

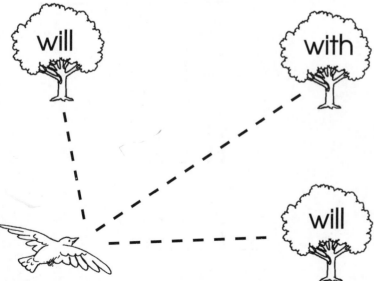

will

with

will

Unscramble the letters to spell **will**.

iwll

_____ _____ _____ _____

lwil

_____ _____ _____ _____

Name _____

yes

Trace.

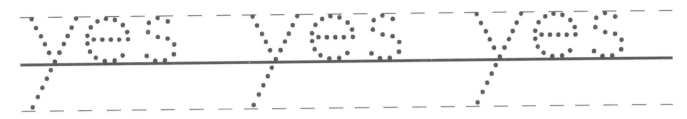

Find each **yes**. Color that vase.

Read the sentence. Circle **yes**.

I said yes to feeding the class pet.

Do More! Write the missing letters to spell **yes**.

y ___ s

___ e ___

y ___ ___

Name _____

yes

Write.

yes

Write **yes** in each sentence.

I say _____ to ice cream!

He said _____, the bird talks.

Help the chick find each nest that has **yes**. Trace that path.

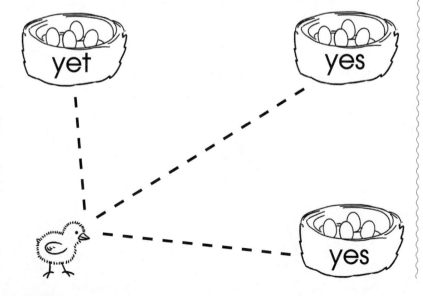

yet

yes

yes

Do More! Unscramble the letters to spell **yes**.

sey

____ ____ ____

eys

____ ____ ____

Name _____

Trace.

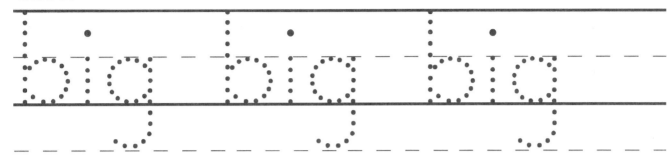

Find each **big**. Color that truck.

Read the sentence. Circle **big**.

The cow went to the big barn.

Do More! Write the missing letters to spell **big**.

___ig

___i___

b_____

Name _____

Write.

big

Write **big** in each sentence.

The bird sat in a _____ tree.

We swam in the _____ lake.

Help each butterfly that has **big** get to the flower. Trace that path.

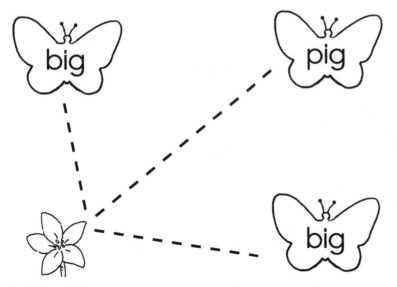

Do More! Unscramble the letters to spell **big**.

igb

_____

gib

_____

Name _____

Trace.

Find each **went**. Color that pig.

Read the sentence. Circle **went**.

I went to school on
my bike.

Do More! Write the
missing letters to spell **went**.

we_____

___e___t

_____nt

Name _____

Write.

went

Write **went** in each sentence.

We _____ out to see the stars.

I _____ to bed at ten.

Help each whale that has **went** get to the water. Trace that path.

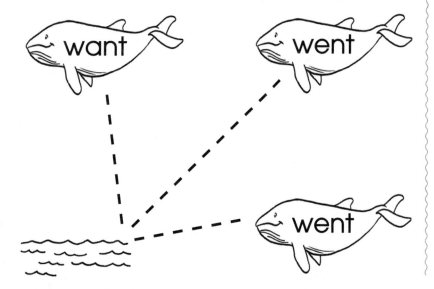

Do More! Unscramble the letters to spell **went**.

| nwet |

_____

| tewn |

_____

Name _____

Trace.

are are are

Find each **are**. Color that boot.

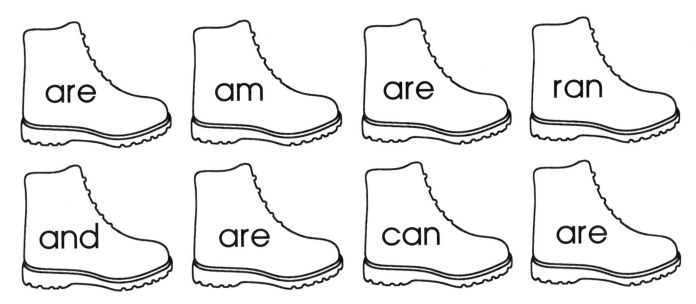

are   am   are   ran

and   are   can   are

Read the sentence. Circle **are**.

Lions are big and loud!

Do More! Write the missing letters to spell **are**.

ar____

____re

a____e

Name _____

Write.

are

Write **are** in each sentence.

The rabbits _____ eating grass.

We _____ as quiet as mice.

Help the bear find each berry that has **are**. Trace that path.

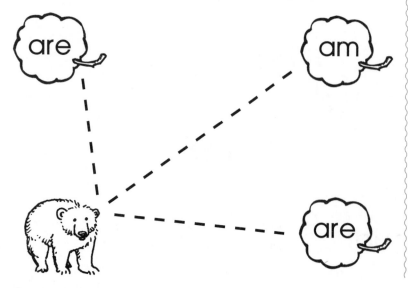

are

am

are

Do More! Unscramble the letters to spell **are**.

rea

___ ___ ___

ear

___ ___ ___

Name _____

Trace.

Find each **come**. Color that shell.

come   came   can   come

come   some   come   none

Read the sentence. Circle **come**.

Come, look at all the butterflies!

Do More! Write the missing letters to spell **come**.

___ o m e

c ___ m ___

c ___ ___ e

Name _____   **come**

Write.

come

Write **come** in each sentence.

Please _____ to the park now.

Can you _____ to my house?

Help the monkey find each tree that has **come**. Trace that path.

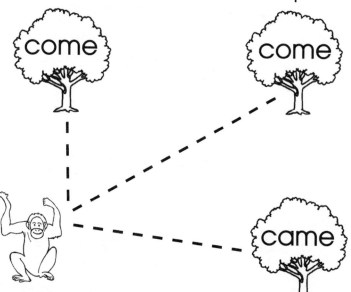

Do More! Unscramble the letters to spell **come**.

mcoe

_____

ecmo

_____

Name _____

Trace.

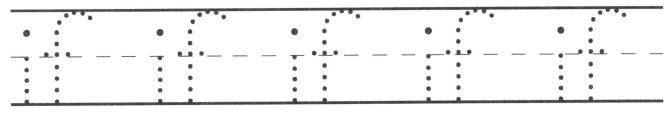

Find each **if**. Color that strawberry.

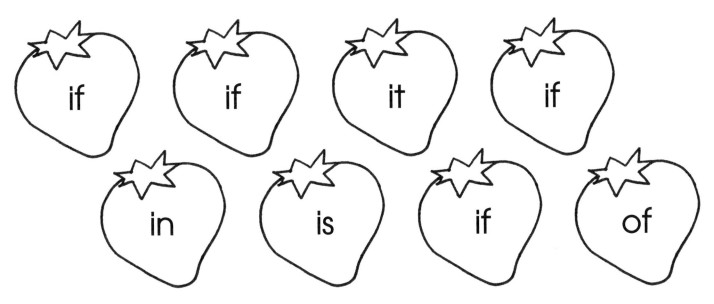

if   if   it   if

in   is   if   of

Read the sentence. Circle **if**.

Have a cupcake, if you want one.

Do More! Write the missing letters to spell **if**.

___ f   i ___

___ f   i ___

i ___   ___ f

Name _____

Write.

if

Write **if** in each sentence.

See _____ the ball hits the goal.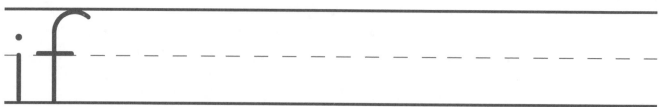

I have an umbrella, _____ it rains.

Help the fox find each box that has **if**. Trace that path.

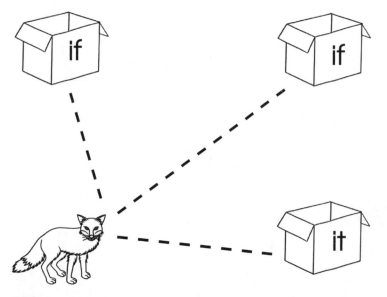

Do More! Color each ladybug that spells **if**.

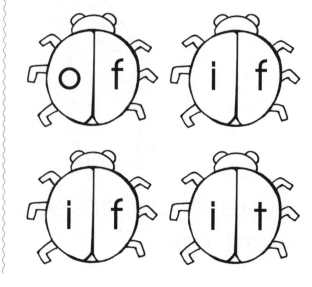

Name _____

Trace.

now   now

Find each **now**. Color that snail.

not   now   how   now

won   now   own   now

Read the sentence. Circle **now**.

The flowers are in the vase now.

Do More! Write the missing letters to spell **now**.

n o ___

___ o w

n ___ w

Name _____

Write.

now

Write **now** in each sentence.

The train is coming _____!

I see the tiger _____.

Help the mouse find each cheese that has **now**. Trace that path.

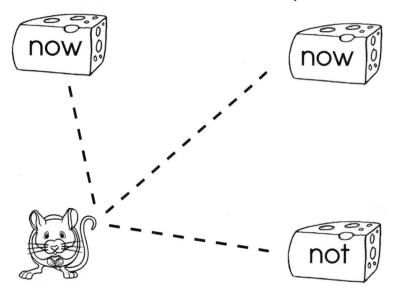

Do More! Unscramble the letters to spell **now**.

own

_____

won

_____

Name _____

Trace.

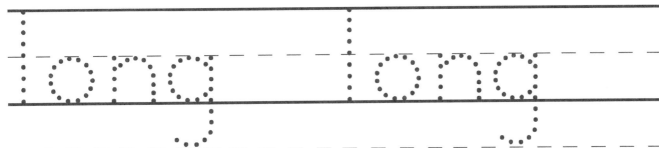

Find each **long**. Color that boat.

long   got   lone   long

long   love   long   long

Read the sentence. Circle each **long**.

Her kite has a long, long string.

Do More! Write the missing letters to spell **long**.

lo_____

_____ng

l___n___

Name _____

Write.

long

Write **long** in each sentence.

Did you see that _____ snake?

The monkey has _____ arms.

Help the bee find each flower that has **long**. Trace that path.

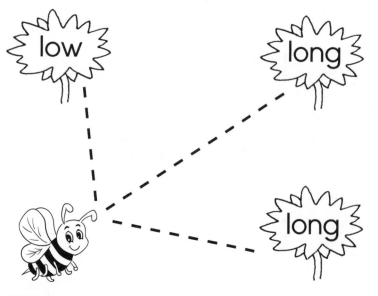

Do More! Unscramble the letters to spell **long**.

ongl

___ ___ ___ ___

glon

___ ___ ___ ___

Name _____   **no**

Trace.

Find each **no**. Color that log.

no   to   on   no

of   do   no

no

Read the sentence. Circle **no**.

Do More! Write the missing letters to spell **no**.

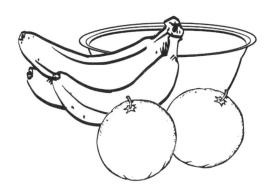

There are no more apples.

___o   n___

___o   n___

n___   ___o

no

Write.

_____

no

Write **no** in each sentence.

There is _____ juice in my cup.

I have _____ money in my bank.

Help the kid find each apple that has **no**. Trace that path.

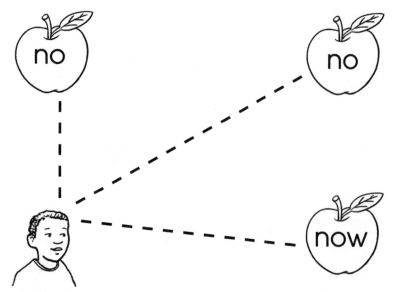

Do More! Color each bell that spells **no**.

Name _____

Trace.

Find each **came**. Color that pan.

same   come   came   came

game   came   can   came

Read the sentence. Circle **came**.

The sheep came out of the pen.

Do More! Write the missing letters to spell **came**.

c a ___ e

_____ me

c ___ m ___

Name _____

came

Write.

came

Write **came** in each sentence.

We _____ to get the pizza.

The squirrel _____ out to eat.

Help the sheep find each haystack that has **came**. Trace that path.

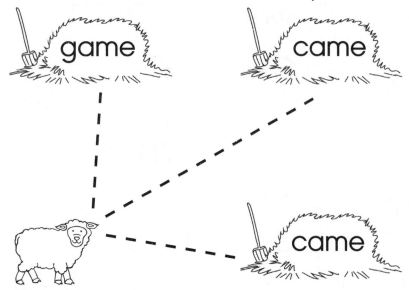

game   came

came

Do More! Unscramble the letters to spell **came**.

mcea

__ __ __ __

acme

__ __ __ __

Name _____

Trace.

Find each **ask**. Color that hen.

ask   ask   as   are

all   ask   and   ask

Read the sentence. Circle **ask**.

He will ask for all of
our tickets.

Do More! Write the
missing letters to spell **ask**.

a ___ k

___ s ___

a s ___

Name _____

Write.

ask

Write **ask** in each sentence.

I will _____ Dad for an apple.

Please _____ her for glue.

Help the man find each truck
that has **ask**. Trace that path.

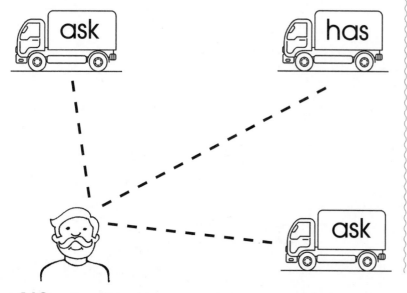

Do More! Unscramble
the letters to spell **ask**.

k a s

_ _ _

sak

_ _ _

Name _____

very

Trace.

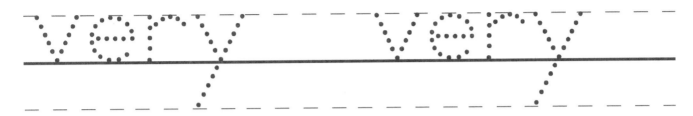

Find each **very**. Color that bus.

very

every

very

over

were

very

ever

very

Read the sentence. Circle **very**.

The buildings in the city are very tall.

Do More! Write the missing letters to spell **very**.

ve___y

___e___y

v_____y

Name _____

very

Write.

very _____

Write **very** in each sentence.

An elephant is _____ big!

This is a _____ slow turtle.

Help the rabbit find each stump
that has **very**. Trace that path.

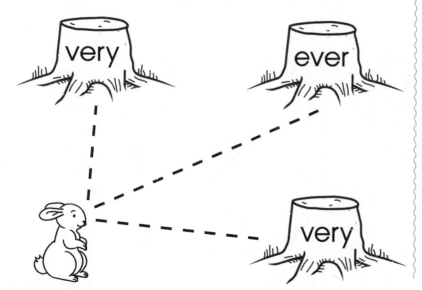

Do More! Unscramble
the letters to spell **very**.

yrev

_ _ _ _

ryve

_ _ _ _

Name _____

Trace.

Find each **an**. Color that owl.

any	and	an	an
man	an	am	an

Read the sentence. Circle **an**.

I need an egg for
my cake.

Do More! Write the
missing letters to spell **an**.

a___	___n
___n	a___
a___	___n

Name _____

an

Write.

an

Write **an** in each sentence.

We saw _____ ape at the zoo.

There is _____ ant on my foot.

Help each fish that has **an** get to the fishbowl. Trace that path.

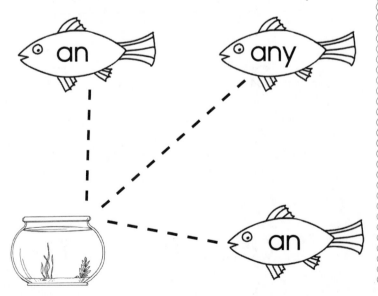

Do More! Color each book that spells **an**.

a n   a m

a s   a n

Name _____

Trace.

over over

Find each **over**. Color that star.

over

ever

very

over

over

our

very

over

Read the sentence. Circle **over**.

The frog jumped over
a rock.

Do More! Write the
missing letters to spell **over**.

o v ___ r

o ___ ___ r

___ ___ ___ e r

Name _____

over

Write.

over _____

Write **over** in each sentence.

Our plane is _____ the clouds.

A bee flew _____ my head.

Help the deer find each tree that has **over**. Trace that path.

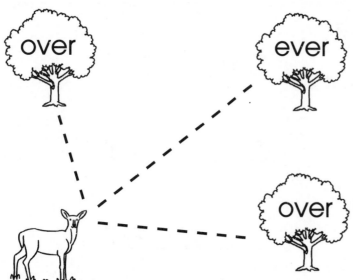

over

ever

over

Do More! Unscramble the letters to spell **over**.

vero

____ ____ ____ ____

eovr

Name _____

Trace.

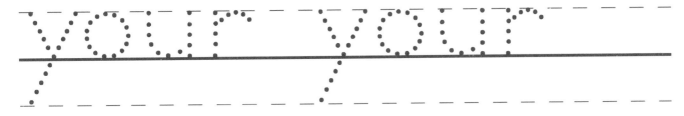

Find each **your**. Color that peach.

Read the sentence. Circle **your**.

It is time to eat your lunch.

Do More! Write the missing letters to spell **your**.

y___ur

y_____r

___our

Name _____

your

Write.

_____

your

Write **your** in each sentence.

I like _____ boots.

Can I use _____ wagon?

Help the kid find each sled that has **your**. Trace that path.

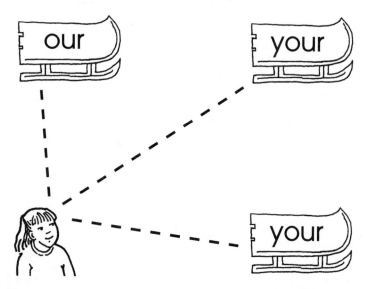

Do More! Unscramble the letters to spell **your**.

uyro

— — — —

ruoy

— — — —

Name _____

Trace.

Find each **its**. Color that cake.

| is | its | it | its |
| its | in | its | his |

Read the sentence. Circle **its**.

My puppy wags its tail
a lot!

Do More! Write the missing letters to spell **its**.

i___s

it___

___ts

Write.

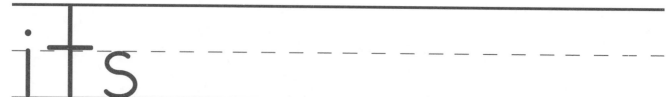

its

Write **its** in each sentence.

The kitten played with _____ toy.

The chick ran to _____ mother.

Help the baby find each bib that has **its**. Trace that path.

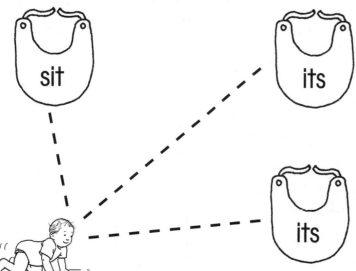

Do More! Unscramble the letters to spell **its**.

sit

_____

tis

_____

Name _____

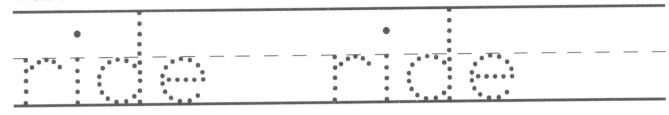

ride

Trace.

r i d e   r i d e

Find each **ride**. Color that jar.

ride   red   side   ride

ride   read   ride   ride

Read the sentence. Circle **ride**.

Would you like to ride
in a rocket?

r i ___ e

r ___ d ___

___ i ___ e

Name _____

Write.

ride

Write **ride** in each sentence.

Let's go _____ the roller coaster.

I want to _____ my new bike.

Help the bug find each stone that has **ride**. Trace that path.

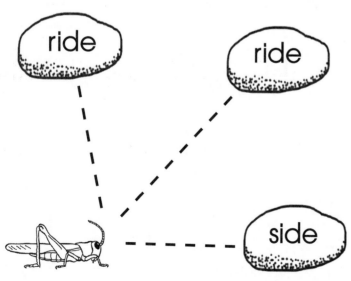

ride

ride

side

Do More! Unscramble the letters to spell **ride**.

edir

_ _ _ _

reid

_ _ _ _

Name _____

into

Trace.

in̈tȯ   in̈tȯ

Find each **into**. Color that top.

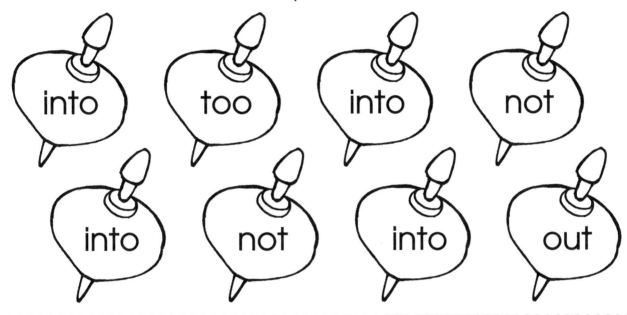

into   too   into   not

into   not   into   out

Read the sentence. Circle **into**.

The kids jumped into the pool.

in_____

_____to

i_____o

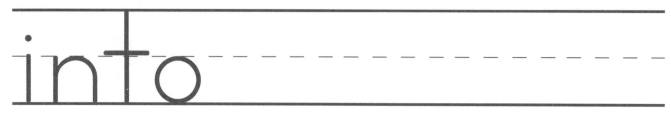

Name _____

into

Write.

into

Write **into** in each sentence.

Our dog ran _____ the house.

The spider went _____ a hole.

Help the ant find each log that has **into**. Trace that path.

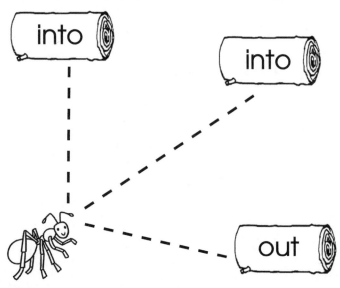

Do More! Unscramble the letters to spell **into**.

toin

_____

nito

_____

just

Trace.

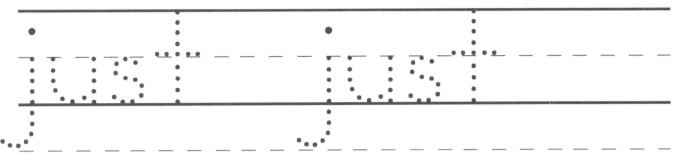

Find each **just**. Color that cup.

Read the sentence. Circle **just**.

The snow has just
started to fall.

Do More! Write the
missing letters to spell **just**.

j___st

___ust

ju_____

Name _____

Write.

just _____

Write **just** in each sentence.

He wants _____ one block.

I _____ found the car keys!

Help the kid find each box that has **just**. Trace that path.

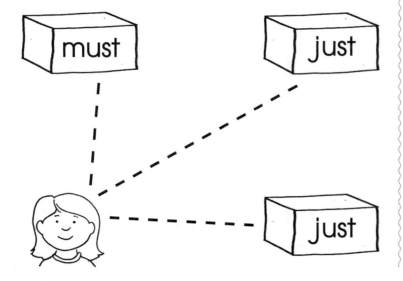

Do More! Unscramble the letters to spell **just**.

sujt

__ __ __ __

tsuj

__ __ __ __

Name _____

blue

Trace.

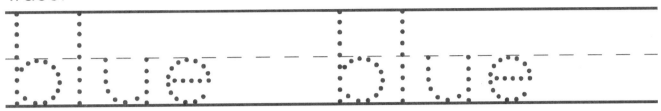

Find each **blue**. Color that computer.

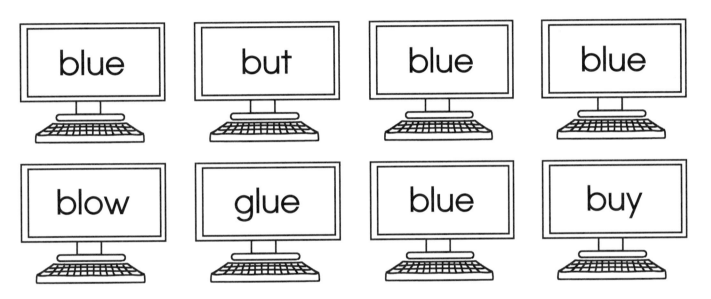

| blue | but | blue | blue |
| blow | glue | blue | buy |

Read the sentence. Circle **blue**.

I will make the
sea blue.

Do More! Write the
missing letters to spell **blue**.

___lue

bl___e

b___u___

Write.

b l u e

Write **blue** in each sentence.

I want a _____ jacket.

The _____ balloon is mine.

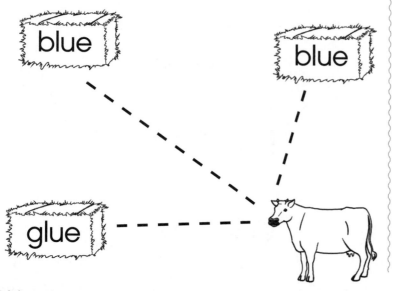

Help the cow find each bale of hay that has **blue**. Trace that path.

blue

blue

glue

Do More! Unscramble the letters to spell **blue**.

bule

_ _ _ _

eulb

_ _ _ _

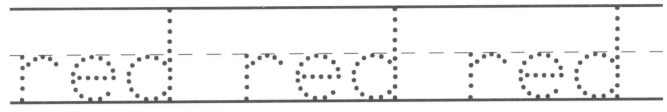

red

Trace.

r̈ëd̈ r̈ëd̈ r̈ëd̈

Find each **red**. Color that yo-yo.

red   red   read   had

her   red   bed   red

Read the sentence. Circle **red**.

We stop when the light is red.

Do More! Write the missing letters to spell **red**.

r ___ d

___ e d

r e ___

red

Write.

red

Write **red** in each sentence.

A _____ car went by.

The clown had a _____ nose.

Help the kid find each jar that has **red**. Trace that path.

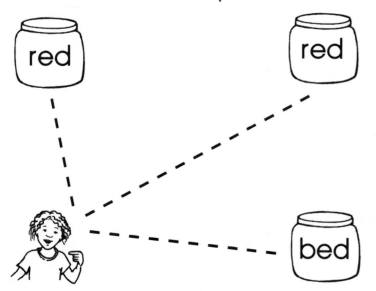

Do More! Unscramble the letters to spell **red**.

| erd |

_____

| der |

_____

Name _____

Trace.

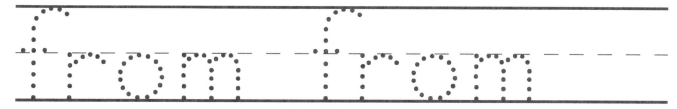

Find each **from**. Color that candle.

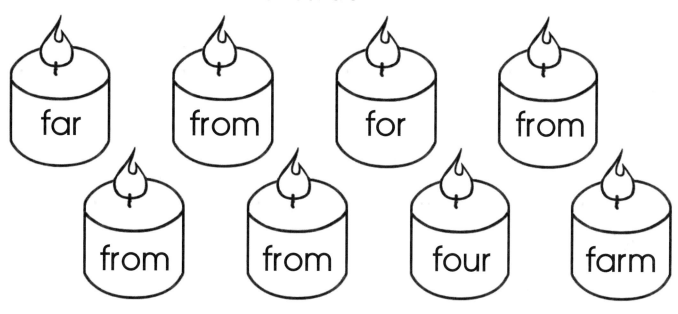

| far | from | for | from |
| from | from | four | farm |

Read the sentence. Circle **from**.

The fish swam away
from the shark.

Do More! Write the
missing letters to spell **from**.

_____ o m

f r _____

f _____ m

Name _____

Write.

Write **from** in each sentence.

We get milk _____ a cow.

I ran home _____ school.

Help the turtle find each log that has **from**. Trace that path.

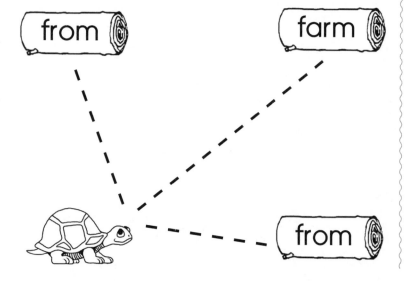

Do More! Unscramble the letters to spell **from**.

form

_____

morf

_____

Name _____

Trace.

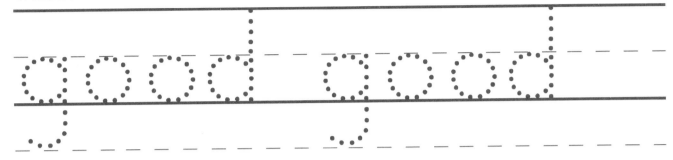

Find each **good**. Color that bed.

good   going   got   good

good   food   good   dog

Read the sentence. Circle **good**.

Do More! Write the missing letters to spell **good**.

g _____ d

_____ o o _____

g _____ o _____

We had a good time at the fair.

Name _____

good

Write.

g o o d

Write **good** in each sentence.

This peach pie is so _____ !

A lion is not a _____ pet.

Help the girl find each bag
that has **good**. Trace that path.

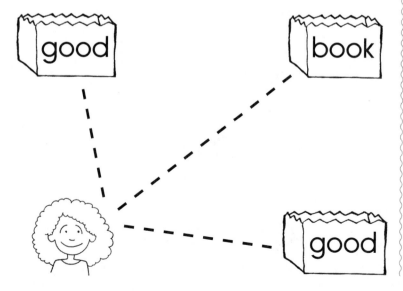

good

book

good

Do More! Unscramble
the letters to spell **good**.

ogod

_ _ _ _

doog

_ _ _ _

Name _____

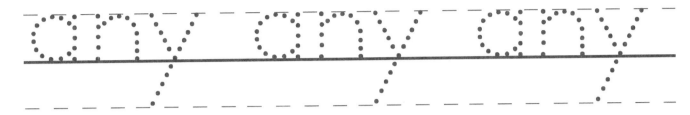

any

Trace.

any any any

Find each **any**. Color that pie.

and

may

any

any

any

way

and

any

Read the sentence. Circle **any**.

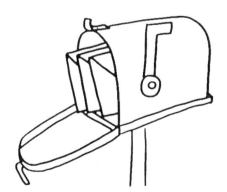

Is there any mail for me?

Do More! Write the missing letters to spell **any**.

an___

___n y

a___y

Name _____

Write.

any

Write **any** in each sentence.

You can have _____ book here.

Are there _____ seeds left?

Help the cow find each barn
that has **any**. Trace that path.

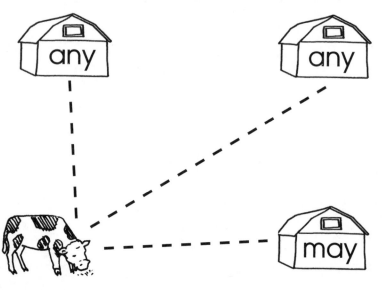

Do More! Unscramble
the letters to spell **any**.

yan

_____

nay

_____

Name _____

Trace.

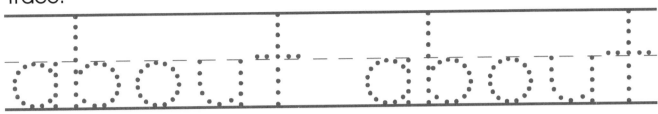

Find each **about**. Color that leaf.

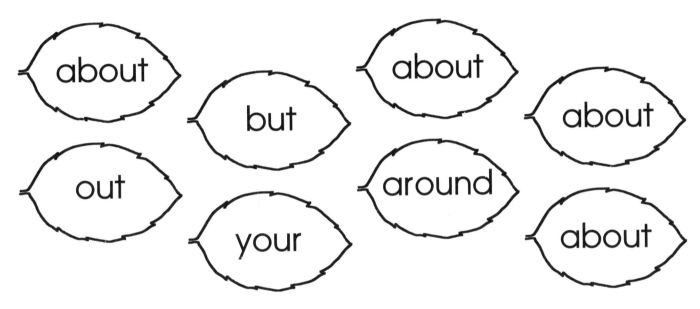

about

but

about

about

out

around

your

about

Read the sentence. Circle **about**.

It's about time to start the bake sale.

Do More! Write the missing letters to spell **about**.

___ bout

ab ___ t

___ bou ___

Name _____

Write.

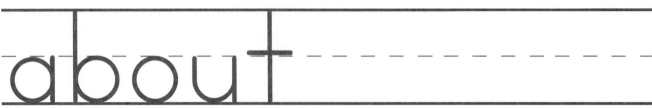

Write **about** in each sentence.

I had a dream _____ school.

I like to write _____ penguins.

Help the girl find each box that has **about**. Trace that path.

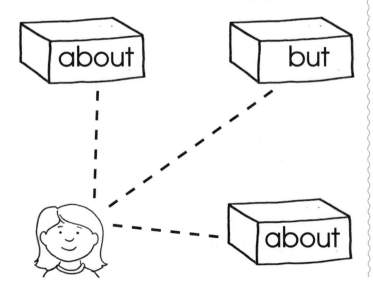

Do More! Unscramble the letters to spell **about**.

otuba

____ ____ ____ ____ ____

aobut

____ ____ ____ ____ ____

Name _____

Trace.

Find each **around**. Color that heart.

around   about   around   round

around   sound   around   ground

Read the sentence. Circle **around**.

We rode a train around the mountain.

Do More! Write the missing letters to spell **around**.

ar _____ nd

_____ ound

arou _____

Name _____

around

Write.

around

Write **around** in each sentence.

Bees flew _____ the flower.

I ran _____ the stump.

Do More! Help the bird find each cloud that has **around**. Trace that path.

around

around

about

Name _____

want

Trace.

Find each **want**. Color that ink bottle.

want   want   went   walk

was   want   what   want

Read the sentence. Circle **want**.

I want to see the spider make a web.

Do More! Write the missing letters to spell **want**.

w___nt

___an___

w_____t

Name _____

want

Write.

want

Write **want** in each sentence.

I _____ a new bat and glove.

Do you _____ to play a game?

Help the horse find each bale of hay that has **want**. Trace that path.

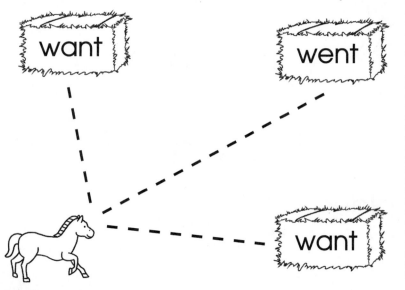

Do More! Unscramble the letters to spell **want**.

twan

_ _ _ _

awtn

_ _ _ _

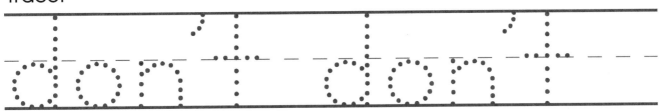

don't

Trace.

don't don't

Find each **don't**. Color that drum.

don't don't does down

don't won't don't done

Read the sentence. Circle **don't**.

I don't have any bugs in my jar.

Do More! Write the missing letters to spell **don't**.

d__n't

d____'t

__on'__

Name _____

don't

Write.

don't

Write **don't** in each sentence.

We _____ have the keys.

They _____ have bikes.

Help the fish find each bowl that has **don't**. Trace that path.

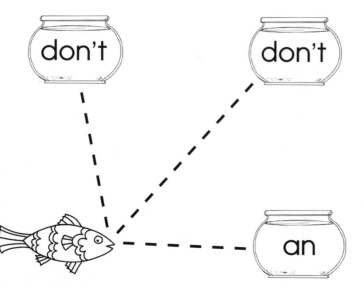

don't   don't

an

Do More! Unscramble the letters to spell **don't**.

ondt

_____ _____ _____ ' _____

todn

_____ _____ _____ ' _____

Name _____

Trace.

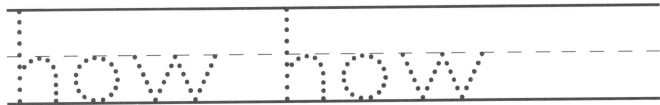

Find each **how**. Color that clam.

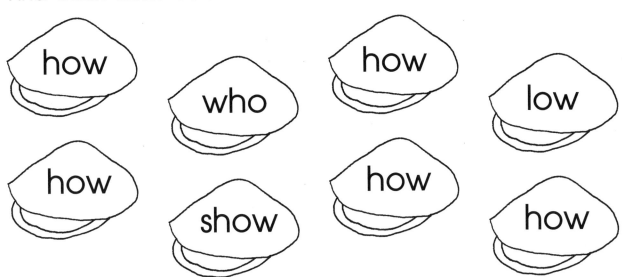

how   who   how   low

how   show   how   how

~~~~~~

Read the sentence. Circle **how**.

Do you see how big
his shoes are?

Do More! Write the
missing letters to spell **how**.

h___w

___o w

ho___

Name _____

Write.

how

Write **how** in each sentence.

I know _____ to swim.

Show me _____ to cook.

Help the caterpillar find each leaf
that has **how**. Trace that path.

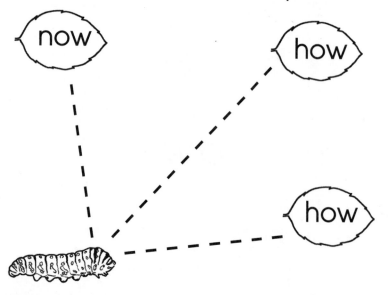

Do More! Unscramble
the letters to spell **how**.

owh

_____

woh

_____

Name _____

Trace.

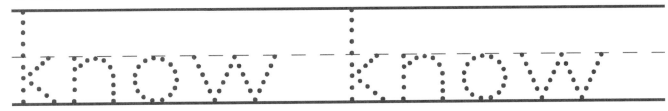

k n o w   k n o w

Find each **know**. Color that cake.

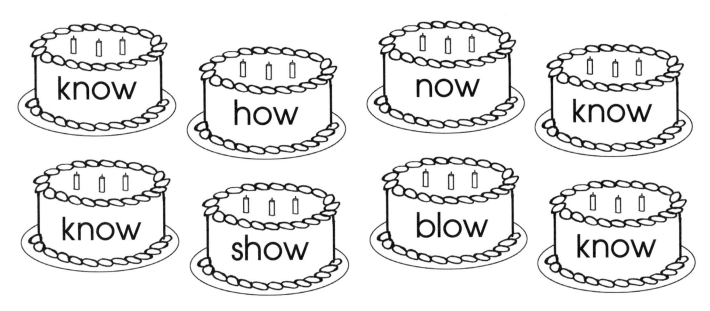

know   how   now   know

know   show   blow   know

Read the sentence. Circle **know**.

We know this food is good for us.

Do More! Write the missing letters to spell **know**.

k n _____

_____ o w

k _____ o _____

Name _____

Write.

know

Write **know** in each sentence.

You _____ I can do this puzzle!

I _____ how to read.

Help the crab find each shell that has **know**. Trace that path.

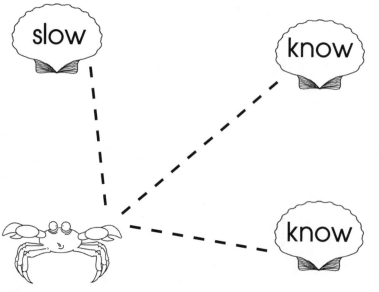

slow

know

know

Do More! Unscramble the letters to spell **know**.

kown

__ __ __ __

wonk

Colossal Collection: Sight Words © Newmark Learning, LLC

Name _____

Trace.

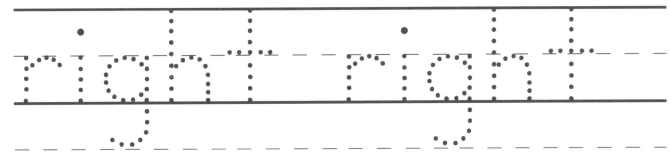

Find each **right**. Color that bowl.

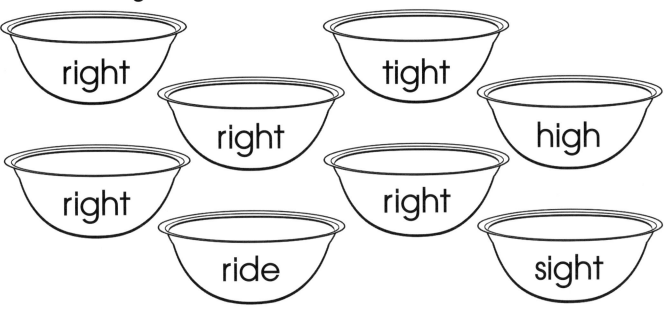

right

tight

right

high

right

right

ride

sight

Read the sentence. Circle **right**.

Put the books right here on the table.

Do More! Write the missing letters to spell **right**.

r___ght

___igh___

r_____t

Name _____

Write.

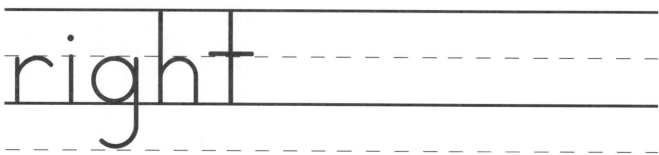

Write **right** in each sentence.

The sun is _____ in my eyes.

Turn _____ at the stop sign.

Help the kid find each book that has **right**. Trace that path.

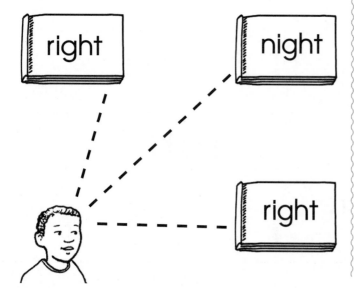

right   night

right

Do More! Unscramble the letters to spell **right**.

griht

_____

tighr

_____

ANSWER KEY

Page 9

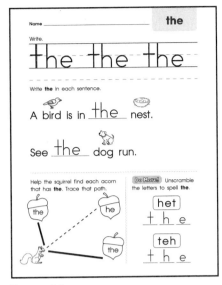

Page 10

Page 11

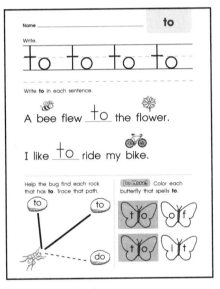

Page 12

Page 13

Page 14

Page 15

Page 16

Page 17

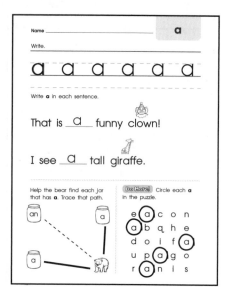

Page 18

Page 19

Page 20

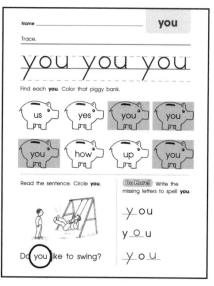

Page 21

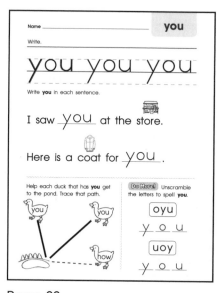

Page 22

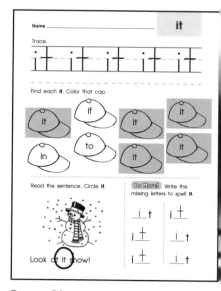

Page 23

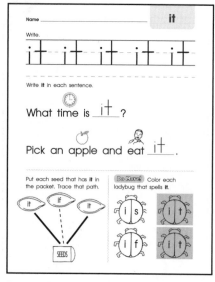

Page 24

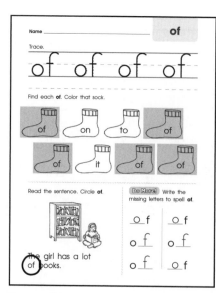

Page 25

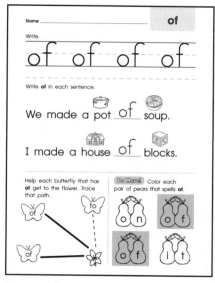

Page 26

Page 27

Page 28

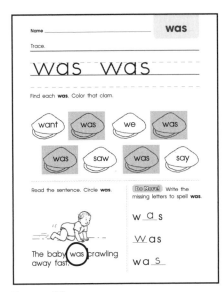

Page 29

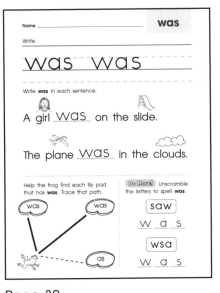

Page 30

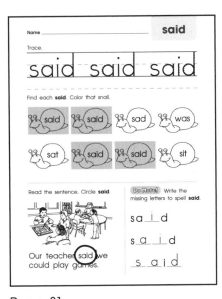

Page 31

Page 32

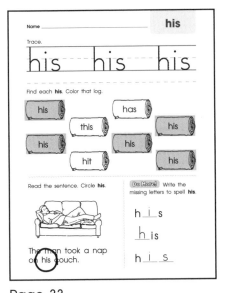

Page 33

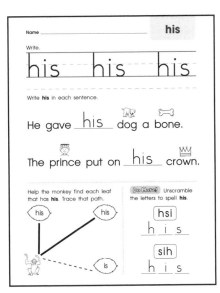

Page 34

Page 35

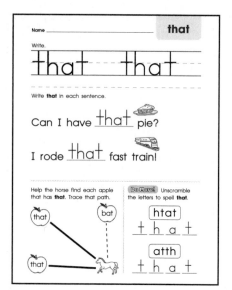

Page 36

Page 37

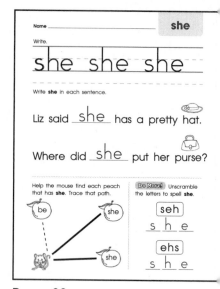

Page 38

Page 39

Page 40

Page 41

Page 42

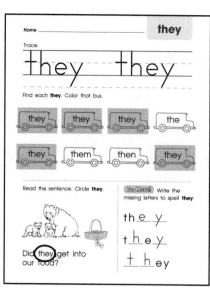

Page 43

Page 44

Page 45

Name _____

but

Trace.

but but but

Find each **but**. Color that yo-yo.

but by but big
but but nut but

Read the sentence. Circle **but**.

I have one cookie, but I will share.

Do More! Write the missing letters to spell **but**.

b_ut
b_u_t
bu_t

Page 46

Name _____

but

Write.

but but but

Write **but** in each sentence.

We have milk ___but___ no cookies.

I saw a fish ___but___ not a shark.

Help the man find each truck that has **but**. Trace that path.

but   nut   but

Do More! Unscramble the letters to spell **but**.

tub
b_u_t
btu
b_u_t

Page 47

Name _____

had

Trace.

had had had

Find each **had**. Color that star.

has had and had
had had bad dad

Read the sentence. Circle **had**.

We had a good time at the zoo.

Do More! Write the missing letters to spell **had**.

h_ad
h_a_d
ha_d

Page 48

Name _____

had

Write.

had had had

Write **had** in each sentence.

I ___had___ lunch at school.

The dog ___had___ a big bone.

Help the rabbit find each stump that has **had**. Trace that path.

had   had   has

Do More! Unscramble the letters to spell **had**.

dah
h_a_d
hda
h_a_d

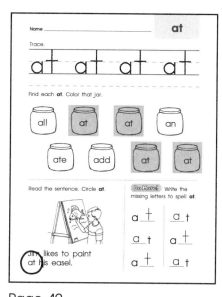

Page 49

Name _____

at

Trace.

at at at at

Find each **at**. Color that jar.

all at at an
ate add at at

Read the sentence. Circle **at**.

Jim likes to paint at his easel.

Do More! Write the missing letters to spell **at**.

a_t a_t
a_t a_t
a_t a_t

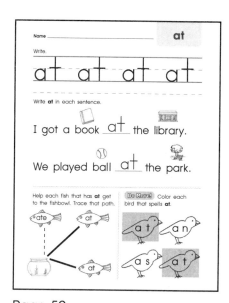

Page 50

Name _____

at

Write.

at at at at

Write **at** in each sentence.

I got a book ___at___ the library.

We played ball ___at___ the park.

Help each fish that has **at** get to the fishbowl. Trace that path.

ate   at   at

Do More! Color each bird that spells **at**.

at an
as at

Page 51

Name _____

him

Trace.

him him him

Find each **him**. Color that cup.

his him he him
him hit him hid

Read the sentence. Circle **him**.

We saw him playing with a yo-yo.

Do More! Write the missing letters to spell **him**.

hi_m
h_im
h_i_m

Page 52

Name _____

him

Write.

him him him

Write **him** in each sentence.

Please give ___him___ some juice.

This wagon is for ___him___.

Help the deer find each tree that has **him**. Trace that path.

his   him   him

Do More! Unscramble the letters to spell **him**.

hmi
h_i_m
mhi
h_i_m

Page 53

Name _____

with

Trace.

with   with

Find each **with**. Color that peach.

with when win with
with will with wish

Read the sentence. Circle **with**.

I took a walk with my dog.

Do More! Write the missing letters to spell **with**.

wi_th
w_i_th
wi_t_h

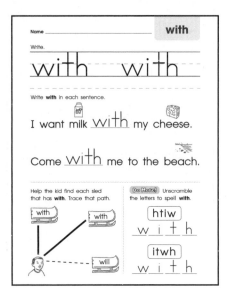

Page 54

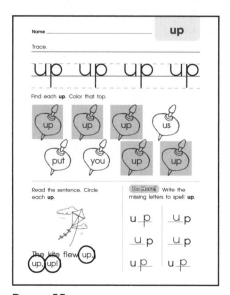

Page 55

Page 56

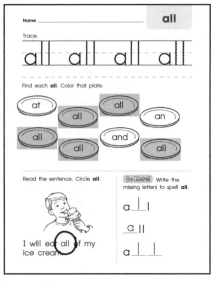

Page 57

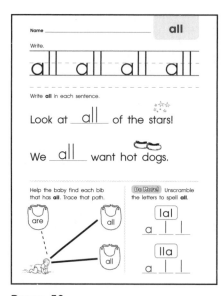

Page 58

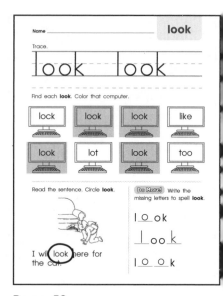

Page 59

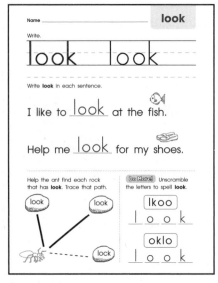

Page 60

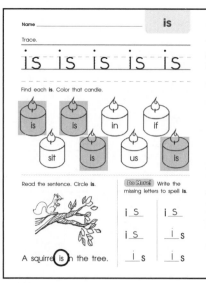

Page 61

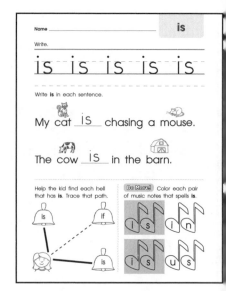

Page 62

Page 63

Page 64

Page 65

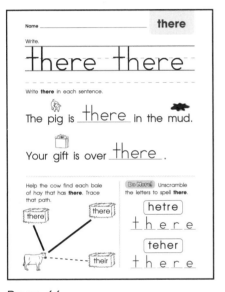

Page 66

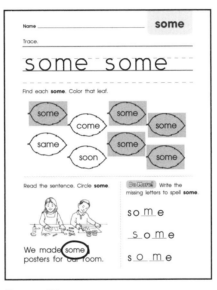

Page 67

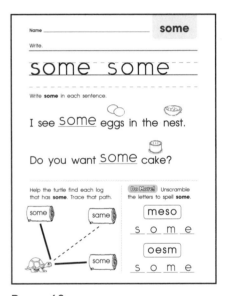

Page 68

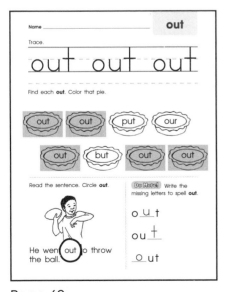

Page 69

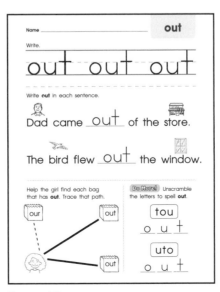

Page 70

Page 71

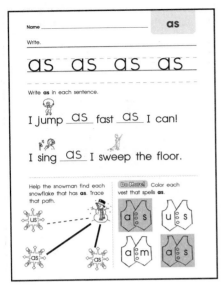

Page 72

Name _____ **as**

Write.

as as as as

Write **as** in each sentence.

I jump _as_ fast _as_ I can!

I sing _as_ I sweep the floor.

Help the snowman find each snowflake that has **as**. Trace that path.

Do More! Color each vest that spells **as**.

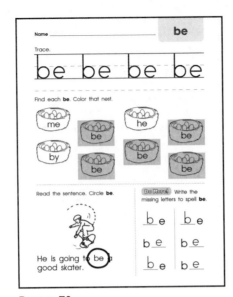

Page 73

Name _____ **be**

Trace.

be be be be

Find each **be**. Color that nest.

me | he
by | be
be | be
be | be

Read the sentence. Circle **be**.

He is going to be a good skater.

Do More! Write the missing letters to spell **be**.

b e | b e
b e | b e
b e | b e

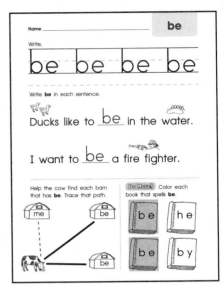

Page 74

Name _____ **be**

Write.

be be be be

Write **be** in each sentence.

Ducks like to _be_ in the water.

I want to _be_ a fire fighter.

Help the cow find each barn that has **be**. Trace that path.

me | be
| be

Do More! Color each book that spells **be**.

b e | h e
b e | b y

Page 75

Name _____ **have**

Trace.

have have

Find each **have**. Color that drum.

have | has | have | have
gave | had | have | hat

Read the sentence. Circle **have**.

I have something to tell you.

Do More! Write the missing letters to spell **have**.

ha v e
h a ve
h a v e

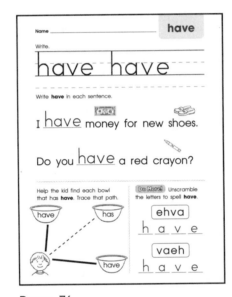

Page 76

Name _____ **have**

Write.

have have

Write **have** in each sentence.

I _have_ money for new shoes.

Do you _have_ a red crayon?

Help the kid find each bowl that has **have**. Trace that path.

have | has
| have

Do More! Unscramble the letters to spell **have**.

ehva
h a v e
vaeh
h a v e

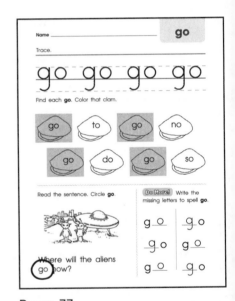

Page 77

Name _____ **go**

Trace.

go go go go

Find each **go**. Color that clam.

go | to | go | no
go | do | go | so

Read the sentence. Circle **go**.

Where will the aliens go now?

Do More! Write the missing letters to spell **go**.

g o | g o
g o | g o
g o | g o

Page 78

Name _____ **go**

Write.

go go go go

Write **go** in each sentence.

We like to _go_ to the farm.

I can _go_ fast on my bike.

Help the caterpillar find each leaf that has **go**. Trace that path.

so | go
| go

Do More! Color each strawberry that spells **go**.

g o | d o
g o | n o

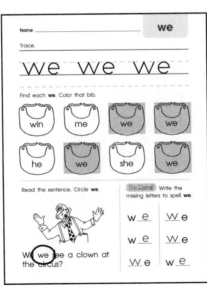

Page 79

Name _____ **we**

Trace.

we we we

Find each **we**. Color that bib.

win | me | we | we
he | we | she | we

Read the sentence. Circle **we**.

Will we see a clown at the circus?

Do More! Write the missing letters to spell **we**.

w e | W e
w e | W e
W e | w e

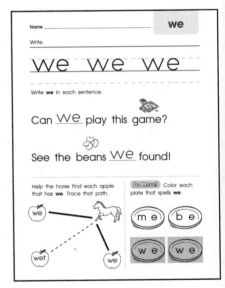

Page 80

Name _____ **we**

Write.

we we we

Write **we** in each sentence.

Can _we_ play this game?

See the beans _we_ found!

Help the horse find each apple that has **we**. Trace that path.

we |
wet | we

Do More! Color each plate that spells **we**.

m e | b e
w e | w e

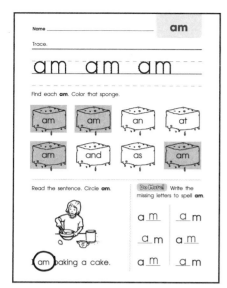

Page 81

Page 82

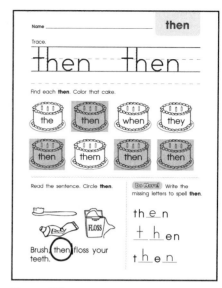

Page 83

Page 84

Page 85

Page 86

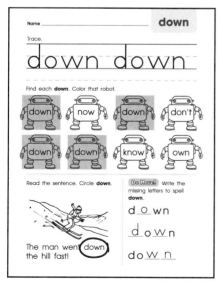

Page 87

Page 88

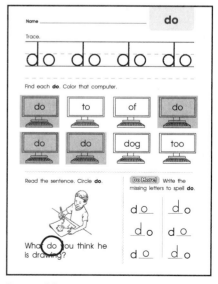

Page 89

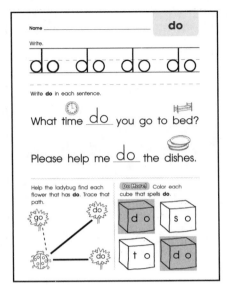

Page 90

Name _____ **do**

Write.

do do do do

Write **do** in each sentence.

What time <u>do</u> you go to bed?

Please help me <u>do</u> the dishes.

Help the ladybug find each flower that has **do**. Trace that path.

go · do · do

Do More! Color each cube that spells **do**.

do · s o
t o · do

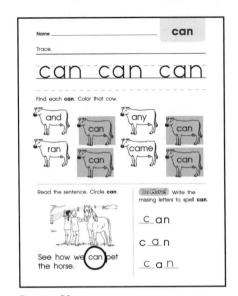

Page 91

Name _____ **can**

Trace.

can can can

Find each **can**. Color that cow.

and · can · any · can
ran · can · came · can

Read the sentence. Circle **can**.

See how we can pet the horse.

Do More! Write the missing letters to spell **can**.

_c_ a n
c _a_ n
c a _n_

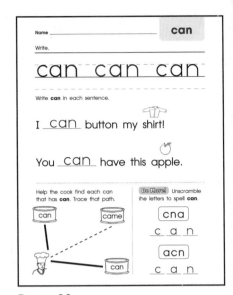

Page 92

Name _____ **can**

Write.

can can can

Write **can** in each sentence.

I <u>can</u> button my shirt!

You <u>can</u> have this apple.

Help the cook find each can that has **can**. Trace that path.

can · came · can

Do More! Unscramble the letters to spell **can**.

cna
c a n
acn
c a n

Page 93

Name _____ **could**

Trace.

could could

Find each **could**. Color that blimp.

would · could · could · cold
could · could · count · told

Read the sentence. Circle **could**.

Mom said we could sleep in the tent.

Do More! Write the missing letters to spell **could**.

c _o_ uld
cou _l_ d
c _o_ uld

Page 94

Name _____ **could**

Write.

could could

Write **could** in each sentence.

I <u>could</u> wear my new hat.

We <u>could</u> have soup tonight.

Help the goat find each haystack that has **could**. Trace that path.

could · could · would

Do More! Unscramble the letters to spell **could**.

dluoc
c o u l d
ocudl
c o u l d

Page 95

Name _____ **when**

Trace.

when when

Find each **when**. Color that cloud.

then · went · when · when
when · where · when · were

Read the sentence. Circle **when**.

We will get on the bus when it comes.

Do More! Write the missing letters to spell **when**.

wh _e_ n
w _h_ en
w _h_ en

Page 96

Name _____ **when**

Write.

when when

Write **when** in each sentence.

Walk the dog <u>when</u> you can.

We play <u>when</u> the sun is out.

Help the bug find each rock that has **when**. Trace that path.

when · when · went

Do More! Unscramble the letters to spell **when**.

henw
w h e n
wehn
w h e n

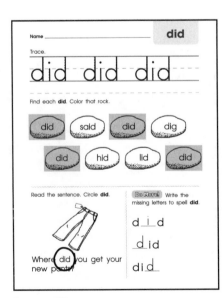

Page 97

Name _____ **did**

Trace.

did did did

Find each **did**. Color that rock.

did · said · did · dig
did · hid · lid · did

Read the sentence. Circle **did**.

Where did you get your new pants?

Do More! Write the missing letters to spell **did**.

d _i_ d
d _i_ d
did

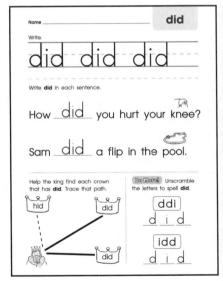

Page 98

Name _____ **did**

Write.

did did did

Write **did** in each sentence.

How <u>did</u> you hurt your knee?

Sam <u>did</u> a flip in the pool.

Help the king find each crown that has **did**. Trace that path.

hid · did · did

Do More! Unscramble the letters to spell **did**.

ddi
d _i_ d
idd
d _i_ d

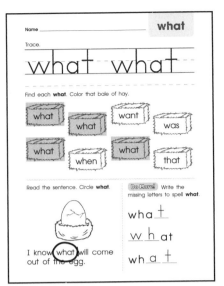

Page 99

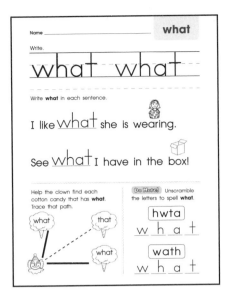

Page 100

Page 101

Page 102

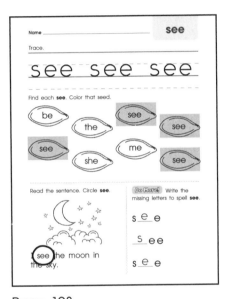

Page 103

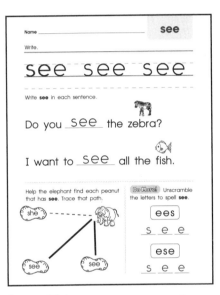

Page 104

Page 105

Page 106

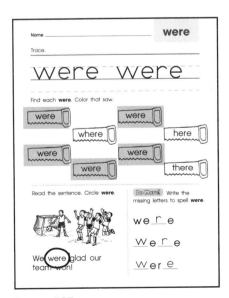

Page 107

Name _____ **were**

Write.

were were

Write **were** in each sentence.

Our dogs were running fast.

The pigs were in the barn.

Help the frog find each log that has **were**. Trace that path.

here / were / were

Do More! Unscramble the letters to spell **were**.

weer
w e r e
rewe
w e r e

Page 108

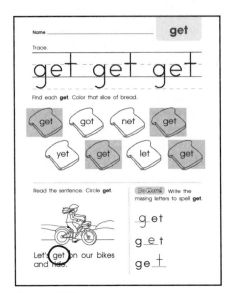

Name _____ **get**

Trace.

get get get

Find each **get**. Color that slice of bread.

get got net get
yet get let get

Read the sentence. Circle **get**.

Let's get on our bikes and ride.

Do More! Write the missing letters to spell **get**.

g e t
g e t
ge t

Page 109

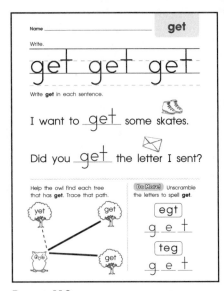

Name _____ **get**

Write.

get get get

Write **get** in each sentence.

I want to get some skates.

Did you get the letter I sent?

Help the owl find each tree that has **get**. Trace that path.

yet / get / get

Do More! Unscramble the letters to spell **get**.

egt
g e t
teg
g e t

Page 110

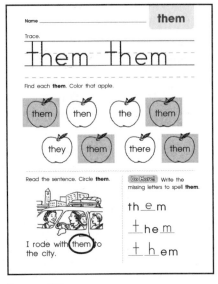

Name _____ **them**

Trace.

them them

Find each **them**. Color that apple.

them then the them
they them there them

Read the sentence. Circle **them**.

I rode with them to the city.

Do More! Write the missing letters to spell **them**.

th e m
t h e m
t h e m

Page 111

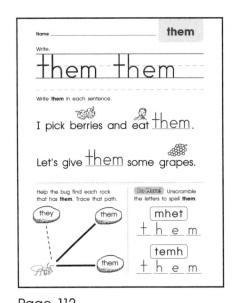

Name _____ **them**

Write.

them them

Write **them** in each sentence.

I pick berries and eat them.

Let's give them some grapes.

Help the bug find each rock that has **them**. Trace that path.

they / them / them

Do More! Unscramble the letters to spell **them**.

mhet
t h e m
temh
t h e m

Page 112

Name _____ **like**

Trace.

like like like

Find each **like**. Color that sheep.

like like lick lit
like live like lid

Read the sentence. Circle **like**.

like to make things with blocks.

Do More! Write the missing letters to spell **like**.

l i k e
l i k e
l i k e

Page 113

Name _____ **like**

Write.

like like like

Write **like** in each sentence.

Do you like pizza or hot dogs?

We like to jump rope.

Color each balloon that has **like**. Trace that string.

like lick like

Do More! Unscramble the letters to spell **like**.

lkie
l i k e
ekil
l i k e

Page 114

Name _____ **one**

Trace.

one one one

Find each **one**. Color that whale.

one none one
on one
one run,
won, one,

Read the sentence. Circle **one**.

We saw one cloud in the sunny sky.

Do More! Write the missing letters to spell **one**.

on e
o n e
o n e

Page 115

Name _____ **one**

Write.

one one one

Write **one** in each sentence.

There is one ball in the box.

I want one cookie.

Help the squirrel find each acorn that has **one**. Trace that path.

one / one / own

Do More! Unscramble the letters to spell **one**.

noe
o n e
eno
o n e

Page 116

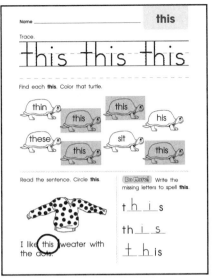

Page 117

Page 118

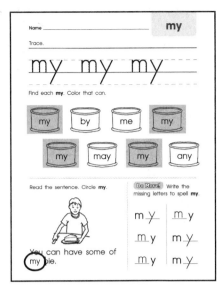

Page 119

Page 120

Page 121

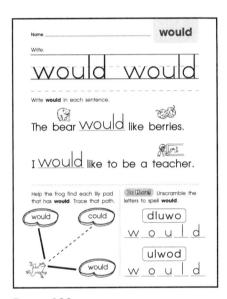

Page 122

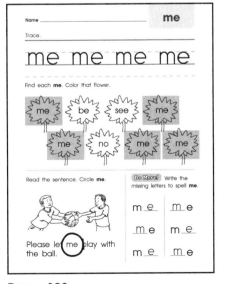

Page 123

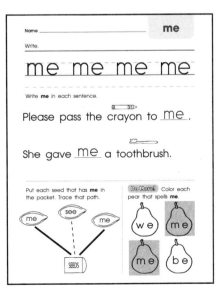

Page 124

Page 125

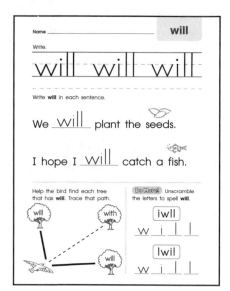

Page 126

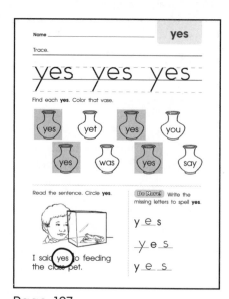

Page 127

Page 128

Page 129

Page 130

Page 131

Page 132

Page 133

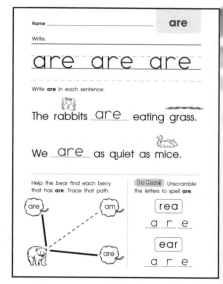

Page 134

Page 135

Name _____

come

Trace.

come come

Find each **come**. Color that shell.

come   came   can   come

come   some   come   none

Read the sentence. Circle **come**.

(Come) look at all the butterflies!

Do More! Write the missing letters to spell **come**.

c_ome
c_o_me
c_o_me

Page 136

Name _____

come

Write.

come come

Write **come** in each sentence.

Please _come_ to the park now.

Can you _come_ to my house?

Help the monkey find each tree that has **come**. Trace that path.

come   come   came

Do More! Unscramble the letters to spell **come**.

mcoe → c o m e
ecmo → c o m e

Page 137

Name _____

if

Trace.

if if if if if

Find each **if**. Color that strawberry.

if   if   It   If

in   is   if   of

Read the sentence. Circle **if**.

Have a cupcake (if) you want one.

Do More! Write the missing letters to spell **if**.

i_f   if
i_f   i_f
i_f   i_f

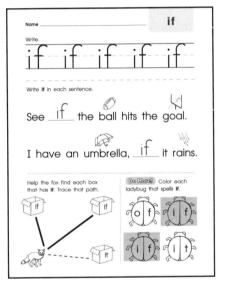

Page 138

Name _____

if

Write.

if if if if if

Write **if** in each sentence.

See _if_ the ball hits the goal.

I have an umbrella, _if_ it rains.

Help the fox find each box that has **if**. Trace that path.

if   if   it

Do More! Color each ladybug that spells **if**.

o f   i f
i f   i t

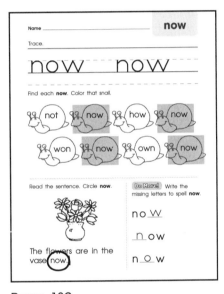

Page 139

Name _____

now

Trace.

now now

Find each **now**. Color that snail.

not   now   how   now

won   now   own   now

Read the sentence. Circle **now**.

The flowers are in the vase (now).

Do More! Write the missing letters to spell **now**.

no_w
n_ow
n_ow

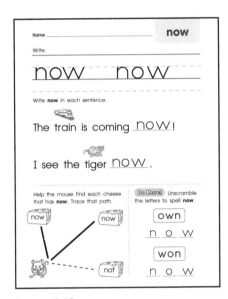

Page 140

Name _____

now

Write.

now now

Write **now** in each sentence.

The train is coming _now_!

I see the tiger _now_.

Help the mouse find each cheese that has **now**. Trace that path.

now   now   not

Do More! Unscramble the letters to spell **now**.

own → n o w
won → n o w

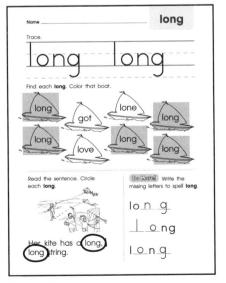

Page 141

Name _____

long

Trace.

long long

Find each **long**. Color that boat.

long   lone   long
long   love   long

Read the sentence. Circle each **long**.

Her kite has a (long) (long) string.

Do More! Write the missing letters to spell **long**.

lo n g
l_ong
l_ong

Page 142

Name _____

long

Write.

long long

Write **long** in each sentence.

Did you see that _long_ snake?

The monkey has _long_ arms.

Help the bee find each flower that has **long**. Trace that path.

low   long   long

Do More! Unscramble the letters to spell **long**.

ongl → l o n g
glon → l o n g

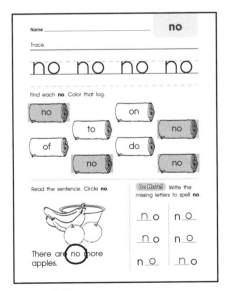

Page 143

Name _____

no

Trace.

no no no no

Find each **no**. Color that log.

no   on
to   no
of   do
no   no

Read the sentence. Circle **no**.

There are (no) more apples.

Do More! Write the missing letters to spell **no**.

n_o   n_o
n_o   n_o
n_o   n_o

Page 144

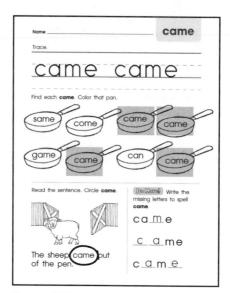

Page 145

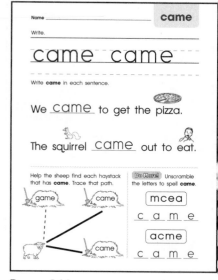

Page 146

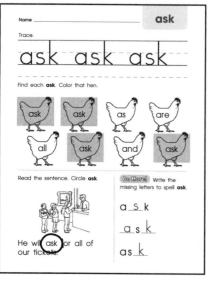

Page 147

Page 148

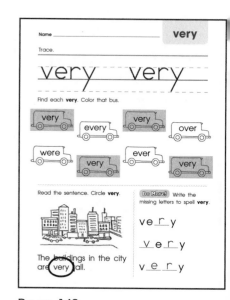

Page 149

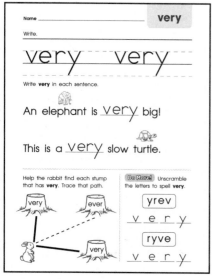

Page 150

Page 151

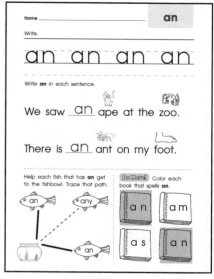

Page 152

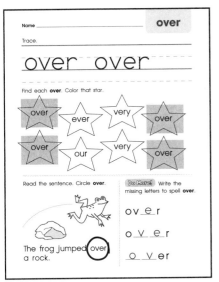

Page 153

Page 154

Page 155

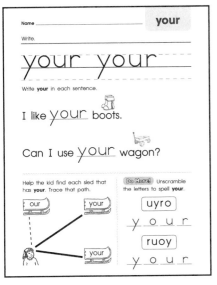

Page 156

Page 157

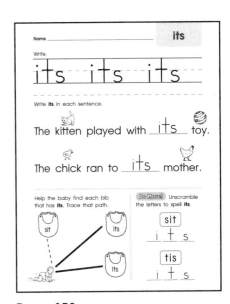

Page 158

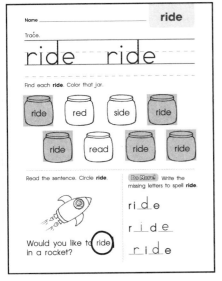

Page 159

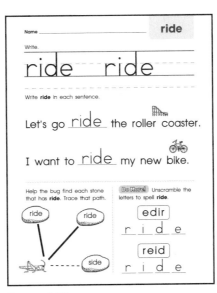

Page 160

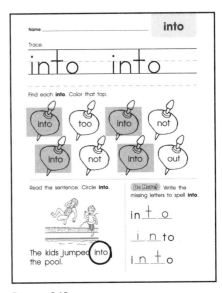

Page 161

Page 162

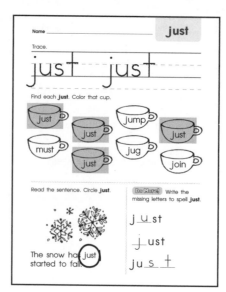

Page 163

Page 164

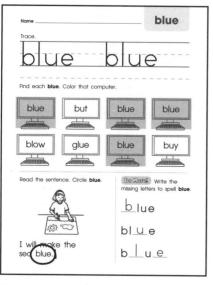

Page 165

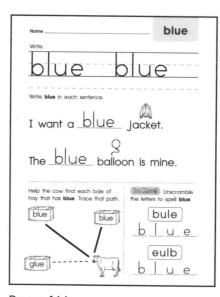

Page 166

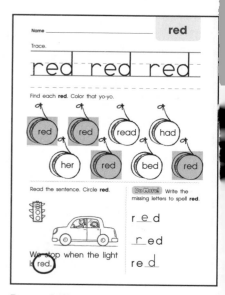

Page 167

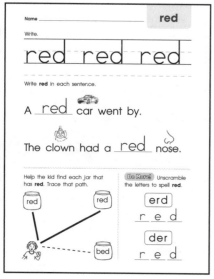

Page 168

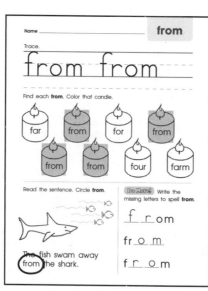

Page 169

Page 170

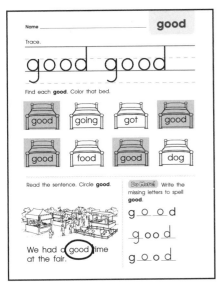

Page 171

Page 172

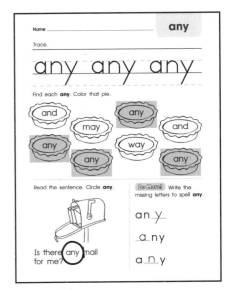

Page 173

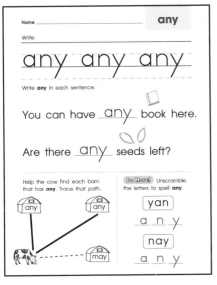

Page 174

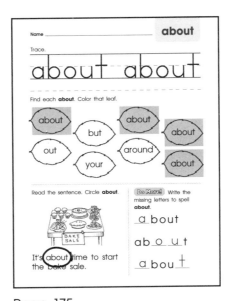

Page 175

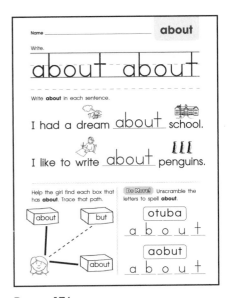

Page 176

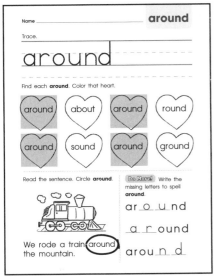

Page 177

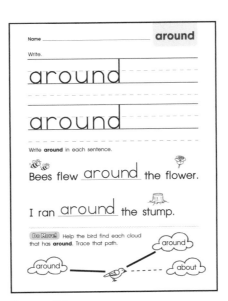

Page 178

Page 179

Page 180

Page 181

Page 182

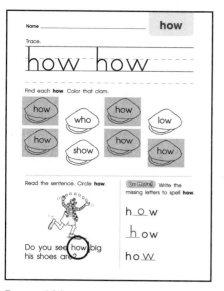

Page 183

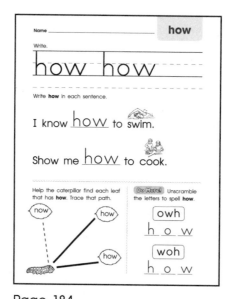

Page 184

Page 185

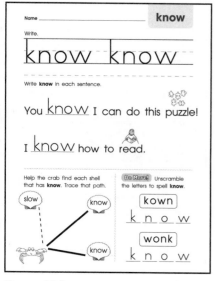

Page 186

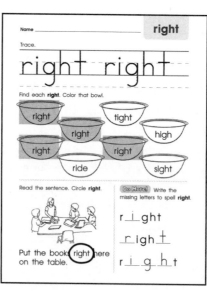

Page 187

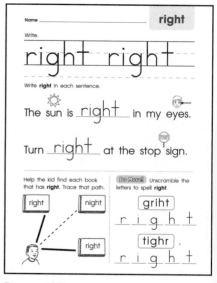

Page 188